IN SEARCH OF THE PITCHER OF NECTAR

SAMARESH BOSE

KALKUT

Translated from the Bengali original *Amrita Kumbher Sandhaney* by Nirmal Kanti Bhattacharjee

THORNBIRD
NIYOGI BOOKS

Published by
NIYOGI BOOKS
Block D, Building No. 77,
Okhla Industrial Area, Phase-I,
New Delhi-110 020, INDIA
Tel: 91-11-26816301, 26818960
Email: niyogibooks@gmail.com
Website: www.niyogibooksindia.com

Editor: Arunima Ghosh
Design: Shashi Bhushan Prasad
Cover design: Pinaki De

ISBN: 978-93-91125-78-3
Publication: 2022

Printed at: Niyogi Offset Pvt. Ltd., New Delhi, India

PREFACE
THE DIVERSITY

I have not seen anything more strange than a human being. I have seen the infinite beauty among this strange creation of God, though I used to think that I would find Him somewhere else beyond humanity.

No man is a single entity. There always lives another being in him. There is one who toils from dawn to dusk for a living; who is constantly engaged in the endless chores of eating, sleeping, copulating and rearing up children; who faces doubts, suspicion, quarrels and fear at every step in this complex world. But in the midst of it all, there is another who is a poet, author, painter, musician or thinker—in other words, who is an aesthete.

He may not be a writer himself, but he laughs and cries on reading a book. He may not be a singer himself, but he loses himself in the melody of a song. A man is very lonely in the ecstatic moment of this feeling. The pain of this loneliness is as deep as the pleasure of this experience.

In this moment of loneliness, the generally homebound mind of a man gets lost in the multitude of humanity. Then he no longer belongs to home, but becomes of others; then he is as much with himself as with the crowd. There is no beckoning of supernatural in it. When this feeling finds a chance to spread in our body, in all our veins and arteries, we take ourselves physically among people in fairs and gatherings. We descend on the road, we travel.

When in a silent and solitary moment, the propitious one has appeared before me, I noticed with pleasure and pain that it was none other than a man. I never had the vision of any other god apart from him. Hence, I always bow before thee, mankind!

Kalkut

IN SEARCH OF THE PITCHER OF NECTAR

Sometimes, I feel our mind is a dangerous machine. Throughout the year, the season changes; with it changes the appearance of this world. How various is this appearance! Sometimes one sees the dry, barren field, with the thousand cracks all around. A crazy wind blows over that hard and broken field. One feels as if the desolate earth is trying to suppress her silent cry. The sky is emitting waves of fire. There are no leaves on the trees, no chirping of the birds. It is as if the whole universe is burning.

Again one sees torrential flood of water coming down from an unseen source. The flakes of cloud are scattered in the sky. The field is flooded with water; her breast is full of green paddy. It is as if a well-loved pregnant wife is laughing and shivering in cold brought by the sudden gush of wind.

I look inside my mind. There is a void there. People say, it is hard to find a soulmate. Is it true? I have never come to an understanding with my mind. We often run after variety with an empty mind. We are crazy about finding something, though we do not know what we are seeking. Someone has said, 'It's futile to search for Him in this earthen Vrindavan.' Someone else has said, 'If you know yourself, you can know the unknown'. And still another has said,

'Whatever I desire, I desire it by mistake

Whatever I get, I do not want it.'

The search for variety is in reality a search for our own mind. In the guise of seeking a man, we seek a compatible mind. So, when a friend asked with a touch of sarcasm, 'Why are you going to the Kumbh-mela? For religious purpose?' I replied, 'Just to see.'

I am not a religious person in the common sense of the term. But I am not anti-religion either. I am like that hero[1] of Manikbabu's story, 'Level Crossing'.

The friend persisted, 'To see what? Lakhs of people blinded by faith?'

Blinded by faith! If lakhs of people are blinded by faith, then why not search for the reason? What is that celestial blinker which can blind lakhs of eyes? I remember an aging Bengali widow. She was sitting on the bridge over the Ganga in Kumbh-mela after finishing her evening ablutions and rituals. Dusk was setting down. I was also going towards the river. Inadvertently, my feet touched her body. I begged her forgiveness and extended my hand towards her. She took my hand, touched my cheek and kissed her fingers as a gesture of affection. Naturally, we talked. I would narrate here one part of that conversation.

1 Manik Bandyopadhyay (1908–1956), one of the leading Bengali novelists of the twentieth century.

She remained silent for a moment and kept gazing at the fair crowd with deep fascination. Then she said, 'Look, the fair is of the people. When I think that I am also one of the lakhs of people here, I feel so ecstatic that tears of happiness roll down my eyes.'

I remember these words now. For, I had also told my friend, 'I don't know if they are blinded by faith, but I am going to see the gathering of people. Our desire for other things may be satiated, but the desire to see and taste humankind is insatiable. What is more strange than humankind in this world?'

My friend was not convinced. His lips curled in ridicule. Then he argued a lot. There is no point describing those arguments now. We are always eager to see and to achieve what we have not seen or achieved. The unknown, and the unfamiliar always beckon us.

True, we keep living with people all the time. We see their different types and forms. But there will be much more people of much more nature and hue in the place where I am going. We see our neighbour year after year, but we may not notice any special trait in him. When we see the same person in a different atmosphere, we are surprised to see a new light falling on him. How strange! In fact, we do not know our mind. So, we constantly look for beauty outside. As the poet said,

I have been observing beauty since birth
And yet my eyes never got tired.[2]

2 This is part of a celebrated quatrain from Vaishnava Padavali, generally ascribed to the mediaeval Bengali poet Chandidas of the 15th century.

Why do we look for beauty in everything? Because we search for our minds. We try to discover our own strangeness in the mirror of the beauty of lakhs of people. This strangeness is the touchstone. Draw a line on it. You will at once know if it is gold or iron.

No, no further delay. My mind is already on the move, now let me move my feet too. Let me dive in the Kumbh—ocean of a lakh of hearts.

I had a *jhola*, a large cloth-bag, on my shoulder and a regular bag on my back. But the sea of multitude at the Howrah station was overwhelming. Still, I managed to get in. The train also started at a point of time.

A small compartment that could accommodate around eight people. A six-member family of Uttar Pradesh, living in Calcutta had occupied two benches. There I also got a little space. Four more persons were seated on the upper berth. What better arrangement did one need?

The lead passenger of the six-member family was a young man. He pushed three large steel trunks near the door facing the platform and flashed me a heroic smile. The meaning was clear, so I had no other alternative but to smile back.

Pointing at my long black overcoat and hat, he told me in Hindi mixed with English, 'You are looking like an army fellow. Just look at the door sternly. Then, nobody will dare to—'

The rest of his statement was clear from his meaningful smile. Thus I was appointed the doorkeeper of this compartment. Perhaps he had his doubt about the efficacy of his own timid looks.

This is our nature. We become unhappy if anyone points it out, but we often indulge in these little bits of acting for petty comfort. Who knows if we do this acting with ourselves too.

In course of conversation, one got to learn that this six-member family originally belonged to Azamgarh of UP. But they lived in Calcutta as their business was there. Present destination was Allahabad, Kumbh-mela. What about me? Well, I was also going to the same destination. Really? Very happy to learn it. The young man climbed upon one of the trunks and covering himself with a blanket, almost immediately started snoring.

The mother of the family, having taken care of her daughter and daughter-in-law, leaned on me without any hesitation and dozed off. I was almost smothered like a sack under her huge bulk. The orchestra of snoring started. No one cared for the glory of my overcoat and the stern *fauji* look. I did not know that even the young women with nice nose rings could snore in such fashion.

Like the fast beat of a ghazal, the express train ran past Bengal border. I pushed my face out of the window. Thousands of tiny lights were shining in the darkness, like the laughing eyes of a child. Lights of Mihijam. Then the industrial city of Chittaranjan at the border of Bengal. As a typical homesick Bengali, my first thought at this juncture was that my motherland was gone. Now I was onto the greater world, towards the great congregation of mankind. That unimagined strange appearance of lakhs of people was calling my every vein and nerve. Who knows what was there on the way.

I turned my face from the window towards the compartment. Everyone was asleep. I was as if the sentry of the night.

Suddenly, I noticed that two skeleton-like hands were trying to peel off an orange with some difficulty. What I had so far thought to be a bundle of blanket at our feet was actually a man inside a blanket. Thin, emaciated body with a lean, bearded face. His deep-set eyes were unnaturally bright. A bunch of amulets were hanging around his collar bone.

As I caught his eyes, he smiled silently. His eyes were also smiling like a mischievous boy's. Inclining his head, he said in Hindi, 'I'll also go, for sure.'

It was addressed to me. My surprised counter-question was automatic, 'Where?'

'At the Kumbh-mela. Why, can't I go?

I was more surprised at the earnestness of his voice. Why could he not go? I became a little suspicious and asked, 'Are you unwell?'

He did not reply immediately, but went on chewing the orange for some time. Then he started talking without my prompting. His monotone became at one with the drone of the moving train. His ancestral house was in the District of Balia in Bihar. He used to work in a factory at a Calcutta suburb. There, he had his wife and children. His wife also worked.

No, I should not miscalculate his age by looking at his present appearance. He was just twenty-eight. His wife was a healthy young woman of twenty-two. She was a kind person and was looking after his need with care and concern. But—

An unbearable pain clouded his sick eyes. He said, 'I cannot bear the agony of this disease any more. Hence, I am going to Kumbh-mela.'

'But why?'

Now it was his turn to be surprised. Looking at me with those sunken eyes with disbelief, he said, 'Don't you know why? Why are you going then? Haven't you heard that the gods hid the bowl of nectar at the Prayag-Sangam[3], to deceive the demons?'

'Yes, I've heard about it.'

He smiled sweetly and asked, 'Why do people from the whole world go there? Why do saints and monks come there to take a dip? Haven't you seen how bright they look? How well-built their physique? People are cured of their diseases and receive a hundred years of lifespan if they bathe in the Sangam at the auspicious Kumbh moment. This is why I am also going.'

While saying so, his skeletal face lit up. Perhaps the excitement of speaking so many words at a time made him breathless. He quickly covered himself with the blanket and lay down. From inside, I heard a rattling sound from his chest along with the rhythmic uttering of God's name.

3 Sangam is the confluence of the three rivers—Ganga, Yamuna and Saraswati—which takes place in Prayag, i.e., modern-day Allahabad.

The compartment was asleep. It was dark outside. The stars in the sky were hazy. The train suddenly changed track with a jerky movement.

Even before I could begin to wonder about the man inside the blanket, he started coughing phlegmatically uttering in between in a choked voice,

'Oh, unbearable pain! Oh God, not now, not yet. It is still far, very far.'

What is very far? I watched him writhing in pain with fear, and asked, 'What are you saying?'

He said, 'Open the door, please open the shackles. Oh God, I am dying. Still very far.'

How could I open the door? There was cold wind outside like whiplashes.

He kept coughing and shouting frantically, 'Open it, Babu. Please open.'

Suddenly, a red stain shone on his blanket. Blood. There was blood on the sides of his lips also. So, it is tuberculosis.

And this man was a passenger in search of the bowl of nectar! He was a seeker of hundred years of lifespan! Oh God, had this train lost its way?

And what about me? I had been musing so many things about the Kumbh, was dreaming so many dreams. But now, the first thought that came to my mind was to run. Thousands of killer germs were swarming in front of my eyes. Run, run. O, the seeker of strangeness, the seeker of nectar, you have stepped on the threshold of Lord Yama by mistake.

Surprisingly, no one bothered. Some passengers expressed disgust at the sound of coughing and turned to the other side. I opened the doors, without knowing that the train had stopped in a station.

I ran to the guard of the train. He said indifferently, 'The train is running twenty minutes late. And who would listen to me at this late hour. Better you change the compartment.'

It was easier said than done. When I returned to the compartment to collect my belongings, scores of new passengers had already climbed into it, finding the door open. It was quite a wrestling match to reach my seat, pick up my things and get down from the compartment.

But the train was about to leave. Like me, there were designated doorkeepers in every compartment. No one would open the doors for me. Finally, I rushed into an upper class compartment. Immediately, a few suspicious half-asleep pair of eyes tried to weigh me up. A few non-Bengali men and women. I had a weapon, the weapon of upper class language. In fluent English I told them, 'I was compelled to board this compartment. Will go up to Allahabad. But will get down at the first opportunity. Will not trouble you at all.'

At times, words work better than appearance. The irritated eyes cleared and started becoming normal. Even a little curiosity lurked in some of them. Finally, a finger compassionately directed my attention to a vacant space in the cushioned seat of the upper class. This unexpected compassion has its value. Why compassion? One can even call it a symptom of civilization. As I took stock of the surroundings, I realized that there were two families travelling in this compartment. Later on, I learnt that one belonged to Andhra, the other to Madhya Pradesh. The gentleman who offered me the seat was from Andhra. They were on a pilgrimage. After visiting the Kalighat temple at Calcutta, they were on their way to the Kumbh-mela of Prayag. Before that, they had visited many other holy places. After Kumbh, they planned to return home. We talked about many things. The gentleman said, 'I have one regret. Could not attend the Kalyani Congress.'

I also had that regret. But for one, you had to let go of the other. The gentleman suddenly asked, 'Why are you going to Prayag?'

They were three brothers. All were quite dark in complexion. All had thick curly black hair. The eldest brother's wife was the only female in the group. She had long black hair tied in a braid that reached down to her knees. There were at least eight ear-rings on her ears and two nose-rings on both sides of the nose. Her head was not covered by the corner of her sari. I guessed that she understood English, because along with the three brothers she was also intently looking at my face to hear my reply.

I felt embarrassed and replied shyly, 'Why, am I not supposed to go?'

'Of course, you can, but modern young people don't actually—'

'Like to go, right? In fact, I am also not going exactly to shave my head or take a dip. Look, our life is spent in a confined space. With the limited scope of living, we repeat our daily habits and argue about big things. How much do we know of our own country? How much have we seen it? Just because I am a young man, how can I remain indifferent to the way in which millions of my countrymen live or gather together, laugh, sing and cry together with their national characteristics? If I feel like laughing, I will laugh and cry. If my head bows down, I would not keep it high in false vanity. And if I can remain detached, so be it. Such a huge country, so many people, so much variety. I came out to see you all. Could not but come.'

The moment I mentioned variety, there was a catch in my throat. That wretched man was there, just a few compartments behind. God knew how he was faring. I could clearly see his agonized face.

I did not know if my little lecture impressed my co-passengers, but obviously they were quite surprised. Perhaps they had more curiosity, but I did not feel like talking any more.

Through the glass-window I could see that the sky was clearing. The crimson colour of the dawn was visible in the east. The train stopped at Mokamaghat station. I got down at the low platform. Gusty wind from the north was chilling my bones even through the overcoat.

The landscape of Bihar was green at this time. The long stretches of the field were full of pea and gram plants. The tips of the stems of tender *arhar* plants were moving to and fro at the wind. Their heads were covered with yellow flowers.

There was a gathering towards the tail of the train. As I approached, a shock was waiting for me. That man was lying on the red gravel-walk. The seeker of nectar. His mouth was open. The eyes were closed. The body was covered in a blanket. As if he was sleeping.

I remembered that childish insistence—'I'll also go.' Why? For remaining alive.

At the beginning of my journey, this was the first scene of death. It was impossible to imagine that Death followed the seeker of nectar to the compartment and was waiting for its opportunity. Perhaps the victim guessed it. That is why he repeatedly lamented, 'Oh God, it's still very far!'

How far? At the doors of every compartment, the Kumbh-passengers were jostling, pushing, shouting. All were restless to reach the destination. But you are left behind half-way. I was also not aware that the Kumbh was that far. Even if I take a thousand dips at the Sangam on your behalf, still the result will not benefit you anymore. You lie here. We rush with our lifespan. This is the law of nature. A very strange law:

So many joys and sorrows come night and day,
Some we forget, some fade way.

Otherwise, how would we have survived! I remembered a half-nut once said, 'They say, three parts of the world comprise water, and one part land. Water is our sorrow, the land—our happiness.'

Is there any other alternative but to remain indifferent to that endless grief? We forget the grief the moment we experience a little joy. I quickly returned to the upper class compartment and picked up my bags. The eldest Andhra brother asked, 'Where are you going?'

I replied, 'I've already caused you enough inconvenience. Let me leave now.'

'Oh, come on, sit here. What's the point of changing compartment now. You can get down straight at Allahabad.'

Perhaps, he was not aware that I had a third class ticket. So, I said, 'How could I, sir? I have a third class ticket.'

But he did not allow me to get off. I felt as if his whole family willed me to stay put. My mention of lower class ticket met with scanty regard. Perhaps, he did not much care about the power of the ticket checker. But I am quite scared of the black-coats, simply because of the possibility of insult. Still, I could not disregard their earnestness and decided to stay in the compartment.

On the other side, the Madhya Pradesh family seemed to have become a little upset at the generosity of Andhra Pradesh. Perhaps, the people of the sea-shore are a little more sentimental than others. The Madhya Pradesh family might consider this sentimentality as a bit of affectation.

On the floor of the compartment, a man was lying with his whole body covered by a blanket. Only the face was exposed. A heap of dry, unkempt hair was spread over his face. It was difficult to gauge his age. I assumed that he was probably the servant of one of the two families.

The train had suddenly switched to a local mode, stopping at every station. After all, it was north India. The nature that I found rosy in the dawn was looking a tad rough and rugged now. As far as one could see, it was only vast uninhabited land mass. Endless harvest of legumes, lentils, *mung* and *arhar* dal reached up to the horizon. Your tired eyes would suddenly encounter a village flashing by. But these villages were not like the villages of Bengal, cool with the shade of mango-jamun-betelnut-coconut trees and wild bushes of *kalkasund*. There were mango orchards though, full of clusters of golden blossoms. And there were palmyra groves. In between them, one could see mud-huts covered with pantiles.

The gentleman from Andhra had been holding forth on some aspect of theology, but my mind was wavering. Suddenly, he said, 'Perhaps you are unable to follow my argument. No, I am not talking of any high philosophy. I was just…,' he stopped abruptly. I realized with embarrassment that my response to him was somewhat half-hearted so far. As he stopped and started shaking his head sadly, I noticed that the other two brothers also sat with their heads bent low. His wife was looking out of the window, but she was not seeing anything. All her attention was towards us. Her eyes were moist. It was as if she managed to force a smile on her sad face with great effort.

Surprised at the sad atmosphere of the room, I quickly said, 'Yes, I remember, you were saying that the Prakrit shlokas in the Upanishads—'

'No, no, I am not even capable of talking about such things. I was just saying that this four-member family of ours is cursed. I am a government employee, so are my brothers. We do not lack money. But we lack one particular thing, for which we have been circumambulating the whole country like mad. That's the instruction of our *kul-guru*, family preceptor.'

While talking, he got excited. In keeping with his progressive excitement, his wife's face was turning red. She was looking at her husband, as if trying to discourage him from further talk with her eyes. The moment she realized that I was watching her, she averted her eyes. It seemed that her lips quivered. Her large and dark south Indian eyes gathered tear drops like pearls. The entire spectrum of light dazzled over the precious stones set on her earrings. Her long braids of unoiled hair spread over her back like a tired cobra.

I could not guess anything of this family drama. Thoroughly intrigued, I kept looking at their faces. The eldest brother perhaps noticed his wife's visual pleading and remained silent for a while. Then he resumed in a low tone, 'You know, Prayag is also called the king of the pilgrimages. This is our last destination. The days of the final test of our hopes and despair are approaching. This time, all our accumulated sins will be washed away. My brothers will be able to marry and my…'

One of the brothers interrupted him here and spoke something in Telugu. Perhaps, it was something about his wife. He also looked at his wife and said something in his own language. But she did not reply.

I was as if the mute spectator of a mystery play. The gentleman tried to smile feebly and said, 'You have mentioned earlier that you are going to the Kumbh to see a lot many things. It is your misfortune that you got to meet someone like me. Please do not mind. What I was telling you was extremely personal.'

I did not hesitate to assure him immediately, 'But I did not understand anything at all.'

He replied, 'Forgive me. My wife is in mental agony. Please visit our camp in the mela. You can find out about us from the panda[4]. We shall be very happy if you come.' Saying so, he offered me a cigarette, as if to mark an end to the conversation. His wife looked at her naïve husband with grateful eyes. She cast a glance towards me also, perhaps as a mark of gratitude for not showing any more curiosity.

I realized that beyond the apparent wealth, prestige and luxury, a huge burden was pressing upon his chest. For a few moments, that burden moved a little, perhaps without his conscious knowledge. He opened his heart to a stranger like me. But he had to restrain himself at a point of time. Hence, two minds could not converse. My only hope was that our exchange on the road would not end on the road. All of us were going to a great congregation. There, we would unite together, before saying the final farewell. At the time of such union, smiles and tears converge. During that commotion created by smiles and tears, I might get another opportunity to hear about his family mystery.

As of now, I could only guess that there was a tragedy lurking in their family. They had been expiating for this tragedy.

4 A designated priest who helps the pilgrims perform different rites and rituals.

The last stage of the expiation was drawing near. Nectar would emerge from the poison. Happiness would fill the family of the three brothers. Lakhs of people were rushing to the Kumbh in search of this bliss. Each had a different desire. I was also going with such a desire in mind. But how far? The high and low peaks of the Vindhyas were visible on the eastern corner of the sky. It was almost noontime.

I felt a little pressure on my feet. Looking down, I found that the erstwhile sleeping fellow was grinning ear to ear at me. He had removed the dry locks of hair from his face. The moment my eyes met his, he raised his palms on his forehead as a gesture of namaskar. I was quite taken aback. Was he not part of any of these two groups?

I asked, 'Do you want to say something?'

He replied in Bengali, 'Give me a bidi.'

Well, the conversation began with soliciting a bidi! But who would not be happy hearing his mother tongue?

I asked, 'How did you get in here?'

He laughed and said, 'I didn't climb in. People pushed me up. Last night when I saw you, I thought this face is known to me. Now, I am proved right.'

'Known face? How come?'

'Why, there are so many people around. Who else has the face of someone from my own land.'

Long live sycophancy! I did not have bidi; so I had no other alternative but to offer him a cigarette. The smile on his dark face turned sweeter. He said, 'Cigarette? Then hold my hand please and let me sit up.'

I could not gauge the connection between my holding his hand and his sitting up.

As I hesitated, he removed the torn blanket from his lower portion. I saw that both his feet were bent back and stuck with his buttock. Even if he could sit up, there was no question of doing so without some support.

I extended my hand. He got up and sat. I said irritably, 'I suppose you were managing well from the street-side. Why, then, hit the road?'

He laughed, 'Street-side? Are you talking of begging? Well, truly speaking, I never begged; just used to lie down by the side of the road. This is a first for me, a journey proper. Pass on the matchbox, please.'

I gave the matchbox, and asked, 'Where are you bound to?'

'Why, where everybody is going. To the Kumbh-mela of Prayag.'

'Where do you hail from?'

'Nadia district. Have you heard of the village Amghata, near Nabadwip? There I sing in the *akhra* of Nakkidasi (Lakshmidasi). I am the lead singer.'

I asked with some trepidation, 'Do the Vaishnavas also go to the Kumbh-mela?'

He touched his folded palms on his forehead and replied, 'Of course, who else is more entitled to go there than the Vaishnavas? It is the Vaishnavas who founded the pilgrimage there. People of other faiths claimed their share much later, almost perforce. Let the Shaivites come, but the land of Prayag would not accept your obeisance unless you have devotion to Vishnu at heart.'

Letting out a stream of smoke through both his mouth and nostrils, he concluded in a conciliatory tone, 'All this is useless quarrel. Let us not waste time over this. For Almighty God, there is no sect or faith or caste. When we are going to Him, what's the point of quarrelling over these petty issues?'

I changed the subject, 'So far, you've managed. But how will you reach there in this condition?'

He laughed. In fact, laughter was almost an integral ornament in his face. But I noticed that he deftly wiped the tears from his eyes behind the thick cigarette smoke. Then he said, 'Babu, my name is Balaram. People call me "mother-slayer Bala". After giving birth to me, my mother kicked the bucket. She could not bear to look at my deformed feet. Anyway, I was waiting with this handicap for the opportunity to move out. Do you want me to lag behind just because I am lame. If necessary, I will walk on my chest like reptiles.'

Having said this, he spontaneously broke into a song:

Oh dear, what game you play!
I wasted away my entire life on the path,
Just because you said you would come.
Now, good-bye to the virtue of waiting,
I would go hither and thither.
You can send the rain and the sun on my head,
Like your blessings.

Like me, everyone in the compartment was taken aback by this sudden outburst of song. But mother-slayer Bala's voice was so sweet and melodious, that all of us were deeply moved. That he was the lead singer of Lakshmidasi's *akhra* could not be doubted anymore.

Perhaps, the song was not over yet. But the huge mustachioed gentleman of Madhya Pradesh barked out, 'So, now you have started singing too!'

Balaram folded his palm and said, 'What do you say, my Lord?'

'You better stop singing.'

Balaram's smile was indefatigable.

'Ok, Babu. No more singing.'

I looked at the Andhra family. They looked at me. We exchanged a meaningful smile.

The eldest brother asked me, 'Do you know this Bengali beggar?'

I replied, 'No, but now I know him.'

Balaram looked towards me, 'Babu!'

'Yes.'

'Babu, the saints and sages spend their entire life without speaking. But we? Since last evening, I had no one to talk to. Now, it is impossible for me to remain silent. Thinking of my comfort, Nakkidasi put me on this dignified compartment. But I would have been happier had she even taken me to hell with her.'

I asked, 'Oh, can't you live without Lakshmidasi?'

Balaram laughed out like a drunk. He said, 'Babu, I

may not have the legs, but I am a human being. So, I cannot live without human beings. If I am compelled to, I provide succour to my soul by singing. I am going to Prayag, the seat of the ever-vigilant Lord Benimadhav. Nakkidasi, you, all are going there. I will be united with all of you again. Saying so, he started singing again, this time in a hushed tone,

You stayed with me for only two days.
At the time of leaving,
Lest I suffer pain,
You took the mirror in your hand,
And said, 'Look, I am at your heart.'

Completing the song, he pointed his finger towards his own breast.

I commented, 'You profess to be a Vaishnavite, but all your songs are like those of the *bauls*.'

Balaram immediately caught my feet with both hands and said, 'Bang on target! You know everything, Babu, everything. In fact, since I learnt that we would be going to the Kumbh, my mind has become like that of a mendicant *baul*. I have heard the call of the road. In fact, all of us are to a some extent, *bauls*. Intoxicated with love; when Radha hits the road, she also turns a *baul*.'

Feeling uncomfortable, I said, 'Okay, let go of my feet.'

'But Babu, you must be a gifted person. Please sing a song or two for me.'

The Balarams of the world are as such mad. If you provoke them further, there is no end to their whims. I quickly replied, 'Don't be stupid, Balaram. I am neither a gifted person nor a singer.'

But I cannot deny that Balaram has swept my dry, urban, materialistic mind in his own stream. He has immersed all my travel-weariness, my petty squabbles about physical comforts and discomforts. He did not at all care for my impressive overcoat, did not give me the due of a dignified gentleman. The handicapped Balaram dragged out my inner self from all the trappings of pomp and glory. I did not know where I would stand if I compared myself with him. Is it only due to blind superstition that the deformed Balaram could laugh and sing so spontaneously and become an avatar of joy? I refused to believe it. This is not the character of a person trapped in a strip of superstitious beliefs. Balaram's mind had been sparked by the pain of deprivation. He is driven by the quest of love. Balaram loves the whole world.

Balaram, however, did not let go of me. He kept humming tunefully,

The dust of the road turned into gold.
Now I will draw patterns with tears.
I won't let you go.

Once he stopped singing, he started talking again, 'I won't keep fussing—how far, how far? The train will stop some time. We all will get down in due course. Isn't it, Babu?' He did not wait for a reply, but started singing again:

Everyone talks of the desire of youthful passion;
Let this youth pass then.
What do I gain from this dark hair, blue dress?
Let my wretched limbs rest at your feet.

We were fortunate that the gentleman from Madhya Pradesh had dozed off. Balaram's low voice did not disturb him. The Andhra family was observing crazy Balaram's antics and more so his temporary patron with rising astonishment.

I said, 'Your first song is pretty good. Who is the composer?'

'Babu, that song belongs to Ataul *baul*.'

I said, 'Let me recite for you a few lines from another song. Its meaning echoes your Ataul—

I won't keep waiting for your visit
I will go out.
The dry petals of the flower are shedding
I have no more time, dear.

Balaram again caught hold of my feet, 'And you said you don't know anything! How could I keep waiting for his visit with my disabled feet forever? I don't have time... Bravo, bravo! Great song, Babu! Who composed it?

Whose song? Did I ever imagine that I would discuss Rabindranath Tagore with mother-slayer Bala on way to Kumbh-mela? And how would I describe Tagore to him?

I softly said, 'The composer is Rabi Thakur.'

Balaram's eyes lit up, 'R-a-b-i Thakur? Wonderful. Tell me Babu, this *baul* belongs to which place?'

Alas! O world-poet, how would I tell Balaram where you belonged to? I gave a monosyllabic reply, 'Calcutta.'

Balaram said, 'Could be. But I must have seen him in the Jaidev-mela of Kenduli. All *bauls* have to congregate there once a year in the full-moon day of Paush[5].'

I knew it was impossible to erase Tagore's imagined *baul*-image from Balaram's heart. And then I thought Balaram was not committing a mistake either. If Tagore had not had a *baul* mind, how could he sing a *baul* song?

Suddenly there was a whirlwind. With a huge uproar, boxes, suitcases, bundles and trunks started falling inside the compartment like a hail storm. There was no scope of protest. There was no scope of even looking at the eye of the storm. Everyone was busy protecting his or her head. In this commotion, a shrill and piercing woman's voice could be heard, 'Shyama! Premavati! *Idhar, idhar mein*—Here, come here. Pull up the old man. Patia! O Patia! The girl has gone deaf. Shyama, yes, yes, you go to the corner.'

Suddenly, I felt a two-kg weight fall on my shoulder. When things settled down a little, I found a huge jute sack

5 The ninth or tenth (varies with the lunar cycle) month of the Hindu calendar (corresponding to December–January); considered auspicious for religious/traditional festivals.

lying near my back. On it, either Shyama or Premavati or Patia was seated. Near her feet, an old doddler was sitting with his head bent down. Near the door, there were two more young and one middle-aged women. I guessed that it was the middle-aged woman who owned that strident voice. All of them were busy organizing their luggage. The woman who was sitting over my shoulder like Mahishasurmardini[6], giggled, perhaps in the joy of climbing into the train and said, '*Bap re!* Good God, boarding a train is not an easy job!'

On the other side, the Madhya Pradesh family was furious and ready for a fight. The Andhra family also was busy guarding its turf.

The train started moving. Then the real battle started. The moment the Madhya Pradesh gentleman said something aggressively, the middle-aged woman in the other group raised her voice to the highest pitch and shouted a volley of daring words, quite challengingly: 'Whether I've a first class or third class ticket, I will board this compartment. Who can stop me? Bring your police or military. Let them beat me or kill me. I will not be left behind. *Arré*, just because I am not rich, am I not entitled to go to a pilgrimage? Only you people will go. Now that I am here, let me see who can touch my hair?'

In between her words, the two young girls were busy managing space for the group. The girl on my shoulder was also young. But there was a limit to my enduring. At the

---

6 Mahishasurmardini is a special form, armed to the teeth, that Goddess Durga took to destroy the formidable Mahishasur, a demon. She is worshipped in Bengal in this form.

same time, I was also wondering why they were going on a pilgrimage with so many young girls in tow. I had seen the opposite practice in Bengal.

I pleaded, 'Hello, there. Please get off my shoulder.'

The girl turned her neck and looked at me. The attitude was something like, 'Look who is speaking!' Then she smiled and said in a clear voice, '*Arré bhai*, everyone is in discomfort. It's not that anybody is suffering alone. Look, people are unnecessarily qurarrelling.'

Saying so, she moved her plump body a little and again bent her neck and smiled at me. This time, the attitude was—'Okay, done, are you happy now?'

It was not much of a relief. I might have to get up and move away after a while. But suddenly, I remembered Balaram.

Where was he? Where was the mother-slayer Bala? I looked at my feet and found that luggage after luggage had piled up to the height of my chest. Had Balaram been smothered under it? I had left one co-passenger dead at Mokamaghat. Would Balaram be the second one?

I could not remain silent and idle. Getting up, I started throwing away the boxes randomly all around the compartment.

My worst fear had come true. Suddenly, Balaram was visible. He was breathing heavily. There was a huge gash on his forehead, blood was oozing out of the wound. He was still laughing. His laughter gave me a bitter feeling this time. Would this man laugh while dying too?

With a grave face, I helped him sit up. As I was throwing away the boxes, members of the new group had reacted threateningly—'*Arré, arré, admi andha hai kya*? Is the man blind? Look, what he has done with our luggage.'

I retorted angrily, 'I think you people are blind. You were about to kill someone.'

Someone? Where was someone? At last, they peeped down and saw Balaram. But Balaram was still laughing with his swollen and injured face. My leaden heart was afire at that smile.

There was total silence for a moment. Then the middle-aged woman warbled slowly. The Shyama-Premavati-Patia group also started tittering. Finding no reason for this jubilation, I kept looking at them with total confusion.

One of them did not laugh. The old man. Putting his loose chin on the top of his stick, he was staring at me. There was irritated curiosity in those eyes under the bushy white eyebrows. His whole body was covered by a shawl even in that late morning. The two deep lines on the two sides of his nose suggested as if he was totally disgusted with this world. The quota of laughter was over in his life. He would not laugh again.

When the laughter subsided, the middle-aged woman spoke first, 'Wretched fellow!'

Another commented, 'Is he a sadhu?'

Still another, 'Perhaps.'

The middle-aged woman said with compassion, 'Shyama, give the poor fellow some paisa.'

The young woman bearing the name Shyama immediately removed an anna[7] from the fold of her waist-cloth and threw it at Balaram's lap. Then the middle-aged woman looked at me and said placatingly, '*Arré bhai*, we have not noticed him. *Gussa na karo*—don't be angry.'

Immediately after that, all of them again started jumping and moving to organize their luggage. Side by side, they were taking care of the old man. Seeing the fuss they made over him, one would think he was a precious jewel for them. Who knew why? At the same time, they cracked some joke in their rustic mother tongue and were all rolling in laughter. Every woman was looking at me from the corner of her eyes. Again, who knew why?

They had not only come like crazy wind. They themselves were crazy. That was the feeling I got from their laughters, deeds and words, as if the caged birds had been set free, as if the forest nymphs had set the forest ablaze with mirth.

Out of the four women, three along with the middle-aged one were wearing traditional heavy gold jewellery. Their garments also suggested a rustic but well-off family. The most prominent feature that would strike one, in the midst of that unbound carefree exultation, was the remarkable glow of their physical health.

The tiger of Madhya Pradesh was still sulking. The peace of the Andhra bastion had also been adequately disturbed,

7 'Anna' was a coin prevalent in India before the Metric system was introduced. It was equivalent to one-sixteenth of a rupee.

though I suspected that they were secretly enjoying the whole episode.

Balaram was handicapped. I had not known him long enough. And yet, I felt irritated by his attitude. How shamelessly he was smiling at me with the coin in his hand! Why should he feel ingratiated to those who hit you first and then throw down a paise as compensation, that too with a lot of merry laughter? Fie, fie upon him! I would not talk to him again.

Not even two minutes had passed. Balaram called again, 'Babu!'

I pretended as if I had not heard him and continued looking in the other direction. But Balaram said in a hushed and happy tone, 'Babu, you must admit that at last, there is a tide in the dry canal. Good God, sitting in this dull high-class compartment for so long, I never felt that I was going to Prayag. Now see, how it is full of mirth and merriment.'

I refused to be drawn into the conversation, but he continued on his own, 'You know, Babu, the real issue is humankind. As long as we live, we cannot do without humankind. Is it possible to enjoy happiness or suffer sadness alone? Then, why so much crying when death approaches? In fear of leaving, right? Let more people come in the cabin. You know, Babu, one who says that I go alone is deluding himself. One takes the voyage for meeting others. Otherwise, why should one travel at all?'

Water would seep through the wall of a mud well. Likewise, Balaram's words were also entering my ears, whether

I wanted to hear them or not. But I was quite surprised by his thoughts. There was a lot of fear, suspicion and narrowness in our mind, because of the insecurity in our life created by petty politics and civic administration. We tread cautiously on the quicksand of life. Yet, given an opportunity we run in search of the pitcher of nectar, to immerse in the variegated resplendent beauty of India. That beauty emanates from lakhs of people's hearts. But what ecstasy this Balaram was experiencing! Was it the faith in his unschooled mind or just the jugglery of words? Did he really have so much love for humanity or was it the love of a four-anna coin?

As I turned around, my eyes fell upon Balaram's swollen forehead. Drops of blood were oozing out of the spot. Yet he was smiling. His unpolluted smiling face reminded me of the Buddhist monks. But such incredible magnanimity was futile in this age.

I asked with an edge in my voice, 'Are not you hurt at all?'

Balaram replied, 'Of course, I am hurt. But on whose shoulder do I weep, Babuji? And what do I gain by weeping? They will say, "We didn't notice you." The matter ends there. But that would not deter me from moving forward. We often get hurt during a journey. Hasn't it ever happened to you, Babu?'

Again, the blossoming of those charming words. But the blossoms had such fragrance that I was short of a reply.

He spoke again, 'Babu, people run their households. There is so much pain, so much hurt in a family life. You suffer in stomach, you suffer in heart. But despite so much pain, tell me, who has stopped living?'

I did not know if there was scope for an argument. I accepted defeat. Balaram again swept me off in his own stream; my scholarship, my intellect—all was easily vanquished by an ordinary handicapped man.

After all this, I felt hesitant in hurting him by raising the question of that four-anna coin. After all, my mind was not as open as his!

For the third time, Balaram's hands touched my feet. Extremely embarrassed, I enquired, 'Yes, Balaram?'

Even he was embarrassed in saying, 'When we reach Allahabad station, please hold my hands for a minute and drag me down on the platform. As you are a lone passenger, I dare make this request.'

As I looked at his eyes, I could see perhaps the real Balaram for the first time. That was the pitiable, helpless look of a deformed man. This was his real form in the mirror of this society. And perhaps, it was this form that had given him such a charming mind, voice, words and melody.

I replied reassuringly, 'Remove your hands from my feet. I will definitely help you climbing down.'

Byas! He started humming a song immediately.

It is often said, once the flood water enters, there is no end to it. The band of Shyama created cracks in the dignity and aristocracy of the upper class. Now at every stoppage, the flood water entered torrentially. Along with the ordinary seekers of piety, this time there were sadhus also. The mass psychology is also such that all run towards the same direction. One did not know what the condition of other compartments was. But here we were, all jostled together. It was simply uproarious. The only one person who was delighted at this turn of events was Balaram.

People often smile, when they feel irritated and helpless. The eldest brother of the Andhra family thus smiled and said, 'Can't help it, right? We are lucky that our destination is not far.'

I replied, 'Yes, all of us have the same destination.'

Maybe, the eldest brother also has a streak of madness like Balaram. He said, 'How can you be so sure? All our physical destination may be one, but all of us are not bound for the same goal. I tread a totally different path.'

Having said so, he fell silent. The same family tragedy was repeatedly featuring in whatever he wanted to say. The more the goal was nearing, his stone-like dark face was showing deep fissures. An avowed traveller on a totally different path, but going to the self-same Prayag!

The condition of the furious but hapless tiger of Madhya Pradesh was spectacular. For some time, the whole family combined to quarrel with the intruders, even threatening them to take action by reporting the matter to the authority.

But who cared? Nobody was bothered by such threats; they had a different kind of fear—fear of not being able to make it to Prayag, though it was so near. Physical fear they had left behind. The way in which they stepped over the head of one or drag another by the hair to create space would suggest that they had even bet their own lives for making this pilgrimage. Everyone was busy about themselves. There was no time to think about the plight of others.

Everyone was engaged in a cruel competition. It was not important who would die or who would be left behind. The only active impulse was—'I need to escape.' His half-lived life was spread in front of him, his long-cherished desires were still unfulfilled. He must survive.

I was unnecessarily hard on the group of Shyama. Now, even in this small compartment, it was impossible to locate them. Even under such pressure, perhaps they were trying to protect that old man. Just as I was trying to protect Balaram.

The condition inside the compartment started becoming unbearable. Is it far yet? No, the train was entering Allahabad city. We were scheduled to reach in the morning, but the train finally stopped at Allahabad at four in the afternoon. Almost immediately, boxes, trunks and tin suitcases started flying through the windows of our compartment on to the platform. A huge uproar erupted as passengers were pressed, pushed, elbowed and stepped upon in the desperate competition for alighting first. Coupled with it, there were jumping and springing of the coolies like monkeys. The microphone was making some announcements in the platform. Thousands of passengers were shouting and running around. The train was Ferozepur Express. The new passengers trying to force themselves into the train confounded the confusion. I looked around.

Balaram sat helplessly touching my knees. I realized that not only would I have to climb down the train with my bags, I would have to drag and pull Balaram down too.

I got up. Hanging my cloth bag from the neck and strapping my other bag on the back, I dragged Balaram up and told him, 'Hang on to my neck and hold on tightly.'

A scared Balaram asked, 'Will you be able to manage, Thakur?[8]'

To Balaram, I had graduated from Babu to Thakur. Maybe, the next stage was Lord.

As I turned towards the doors, all my reasoning left me. I adopted the same behaviour which I had been condemning so far. I jumped forward like a mad buffalo, with total disregard for anyone around.

I heard the anxious voice of the eldest Andhra brother. 'What are you doing, Mister? Listen.'

No, I would not listen. I had to get down. I was not aware how far I had progressed when I heard a sharp cry of agony. It was Shyama. My elbow was pressed into her throat. Her companions were crying and shouting all around, but I could not see anyone properly. She caught hold my elbow with tremendous force. O, God, such a huge burden. I felt I was dying.

Suddenly, a gush of cold wind hit my sweating face. I had landed on the platform. Balaram shook himself free from my neck. He was unscathed. There was praise of the Lord in his voice.

8 Thakur is an honorific address meant for God or great mentors.

Somebody was holding on to my overcoat from behind. I turned around and found that it was Shyama. There were tears in her anxious eyes. She entreated helplessly, 'Please help my people alight, Bengali Babu.'

The same ordeal, again? But by then, two Railway police personnel had arrived. It was the gentleman from Madhya Pradesh who had summoned them. The situation was brought under some control.

Perhaps, service to the others had its own addiction. It obsessed the human mind sometimes. I also became obsessed at that point of time. Handing over my bag to Shyama, I boarded the train again.

On seeing me, the middle-aged woman immediately cried out, 'For God's sake, Babu, take this old man with you. Help him get down.'

Before she could complete her sentence, the doddering old fellow caught hold of me, like a sinking man catching hold of a straw.

Somehow, I managed to climb down with him in toe. Gradually, everyone was on the platform. The cries of agony, frustration and anguish, the pain and hardship—everything was forgotten in a moment.

Shyama was laughing. Gesturing towards me, she was saying something to her group members. Perhaps, she was telling them that they had never seen a better do-gooder than me.

Balaram called, 'Thakur!'

I replied, 'I am a *shudra*[9] by caste, Balaram. Don't call me Thakur.'

But Balaram had a flair for words. He parried, 'But the trait of a proper Thakur is written all over your face. So, I will not take your objection seriously. Thakur, here comes Nakkidasi.'

A few patent Bengali *namavali*-clad Vaishnavas came and surrounded Balaram. With them was a hefty dark woman.

I guessed this was Lakshmidasi of Amghat. She was around forty. She wore *namavali* on her white borderless sari. Her thick lips were smeared with the stain of *paan* and *dokta*. She looked at me with large eyes, but did not say anything. Perhaps, she was dumbstruck with gratitude that I had saved her lead singer.

Finally, I said, 'Ok, it's time to leave, Balaram.'

Lakshmidasi reacted this time. She also addressed me as Thakur and requested, 'Thakur, please visit our ashram whenever you find time.

I looked at her. Even at forty, the large liquid eyes of Lashmidasi were full of curiosity and humility.'

'Where is your ashram?' I asked.

'I don't know. We have never been there. It is called Sri Nandagopal Madhavacharya Babaji's temple. We will also have to find it out.'

I said, 'I'll try. Please don't mind, if I can't make it. But the voice of your lead singer is very sweet. I will like to listen to him singing one day.'

9 In the Indian caste system, *shudras* belong to the lowest strata.

The Andhra family was leaving the platform guided by a liveried driver. All of them smiled at me. The eldest brother reminded me, 'Hope you remember the name of our camp. Must visit one day.'

I moved forward towards the common exit. I knew Balaram was looking at me with teary eyes. Mother-slayer Bala, a genuine friend of humankind. I did not know if I would ever find him again in the huge crowd of this Mahakumbh.

The human mind is like the sand-bank of a river; there is constant accumulation of alluvial deposit there. Footsteps of moments, of seconds, of minutes, of hours, of time and era. In just about half-a-day, the intense memory of a deceased co-passenger had faded from my memory. The same would happen with Balaram also. Some incident in future may rekindle the memory of this pilgrimage to Kumbh-mela, when perhaps the photo album of all these strange people would flash across my mind.

In fact, memory is like a beloved in arms. There is never pure and unmixed happiness in love. It is always an admixture of happiness and grief; hence, salty tears are also an accompaniment to it. Grief is also like that. Though we suffer intolerable pain in remembering a tragic event, we cannot do without such memory also.

The microphone was constantly announcing, 'Do not forget to take the injection for cholera; you have to obtain the certificate after taking the injection. Without the certificate your entry to the mela is not permitted.'

The arrangement for vaccination was also elaborate. The whole station had been converted to a temporary jail by erecting bamboo fences. At every door of this jail, a number of police personnel were deployed. In the open courtyard of the station, there were counters where male and female paramedics were waiting with shining syringe and cotton wool to prevent the epidemic.

Here also, the Shyama brigade had created a ruckus. They would not take injection under any circumstances. Not only Shyama's group, many other such rural groups were sitting in a sort of dharna against the injection drive.

Some of these piety-seekers had been crying out loud, 'O God, O Mahadev, what strange deeds are being done in your kingdom!'

I was astonished to see a well-built, strong young man wiping tears with his pagri.

'Why are you crying?' I asked.

He gave me a vacant look for a few moments and replied in a broken voice, 'They will not allow us in without the injection.'

True, Man is the strangest creation of God! From his appearance, one could guess that the man was a farmer from Rajasthan. His body was four times sturdier than mine. His huge palm could perhaps squeeze me to death. It is to be seen to be believed that he was crying in fear of a needle-prick. And maybe, the same fellow would not think twice in breaking the head of another farmer on the flimsy grounds of a minor land dispute. He would not be scared by the sight of blood at that time. Again, he would easily bear the pain of piercing his nose and ear if it was done in the name of religion. But injection! *That* was dangerous.

But all this hue and cry could not move the cruel injection-god. Without his endorsement the door to heaven remained closed. Those who were scared but intelligent did not waste time. They were quickly finishing the job and entering the fair ground.

The party of Shyama finally offered bribe to the injection-pushers, but even if they were lured by the filthy lucre, they could not perhaps take it in broad daylight. There is something called shame after all. However, I did not waste any more time. After taking the injection and pocketing the certificate, I was about to enter the fairground when Shyama and the middle-aged woman approached me. Behind them, there were Premavati, Patia and the old man.

Shyama asked in an apprehensive tone, 'Did it hurt?'

I thought of replying like Balaram, 'Can you move forward without some hurt?' Instead, I said, 'Very little. Nothing to be afraid of.'

Shyama still persisted, 'Are you telling the truth?'

'What do I gain by telling a lie? Try it for yourself.'

Shyama held my eyes for a few moments with a searching look before asking again, 'Will our old man be able to bear it?'

I reassured her, 'Of course. He can take hundred such injections.'

As I came out with a smiling face, an ageless old Bengali woman confronted me in a stern voice, 'Well, young man, if all of you keep taking the injection with a smile in your face, will those buggers spare us? Was it not your duty to talk to the officials, so that we oldies are exempted?'

I was quite taken aback by this onslaught.

With bewilderment in my voice, I asked, 'Are you talking to me?'

'Who else?'

'But whom shall I talk to and convince?'

'Why, tell those Hindiwalas that we are at the fag end of our life. If we die of the epidemic, let it be. But it is not possible for us to take those *ingison-fingison*!'

Thank God, I had not committed any serious crime. A young man of around thirty was standing near the old woman. He had already wrapped himself with a shawl. It was cold, but not so cold as to cover oneself completely with woollens. As a matter of fact, I had to take off my coat because of the warmth created by the crowd.

I noticed a very young girl standing by the young man. Her face was covered by the corner of her sari. She also had an anxious look. As he caught my eyes, the man asked, 'Please advise what we should do.'

I counter-questioned, 'Have you also not taken the injection?'

The man was not ashamed at all. He said in a distressed voice. 'Well, a little scared, you know. I never had the occasion to take it. And my wife here is desperate not to take it. And you have heard Didima.'

I was not aware that a mere injection still evoked so much fear in this country.

I said, 'But you knew about it beforehand. Why didn't you make some arrangement to avoid it, then?'

The moment I said this, the young man flared up. He shouted, 'Sir, it is all because of this old foggy. I told her repeatedly to give me six rupees. I would have paid two rupees each to the Municipal Health officers and obtained the certificate. But the stingy woman would not spare the money. Now, who will help you cross this Baitarani[10]?'

But Didima was not to be cowed down easily. She shouted back, 'O you good-for-nothing. You can't even earn two paise, and ask for six rupees! And did I know at that time that these buggers would harass us like this?'

The young man was further incensed. He took off the shawl and tied it around his waste. Then he declared, 'I will go and take the injection. Do whatever you want to do.'

It was quite a showdown. The woman became wild with rage. She shouted, 'Then I will hit my head on the floor and die right here. I am warning, you, Pellad. Don't go for the injection.'

But Prahlad also did not lag behind in bravado. He said, 'You may die, but I am going to take the injection.'

So he declared, but would not proceed towards the injection booth.

---

10 Baitarani is an imaginary mythic river that divides heaven from earth in Hindu mythology. One has to cross this river to reach the other world. It is parallel to the Greek mythological river, Lithe.

Had I ever thought that I would witness such a typically sentimental Bengali family drama at the Allahabad station in north India! There were many other onlookers. Perhaps, men and women from all other states of India watched this melodrama.

I did not stay on to see the curtain of this drama, as volunteers of the epidemic camp asked for dispersement of the crowd. I had no other alternative but to move on.

So, this is the city of Allahabad. Prayag of the ancient Indian kingdom. Today, only the Sangam area bears the radiant glory of the name 'Prayag', the paradise of Hindu pilgrimage. But once upon a time, the name invoked the essence of a vast kingdom, whose story would enthral not only a religious Hindu, but every history-buff worth his salt.

Here, cycle rickshaws do not have ear-splitting horns, but only 'cring-cring' bells, which sounded like the warbling laughter of a bevy of girls. The rickshawalas were speeding away towards their destination. Today, they did not have time to spare, as rickshaws were at a premium. They could charge four times the usual fare, yet there would be no dearth of passengers. Today, demand was much more than supply.

The city of Allahabad bears a close resemblance with the city of Dacca, the capital of East Pakistan.[11] Pitched roads were lined with pukka houses on both sides. Buses, lorries and private cars were rushing past, raising a trail of dust. Then there were cycle rickshaws and a variety of tongas.

11 Presently the capital of Bangladesh and spelt as Dhaka.

Perhaps these tongas bore the memory of horse-drawn carriages of ancient India.

Time passes. One era gives way to another. While passing, it leaves its mark. All milestones of history are human achievements. It is humankind who builds and it is humankind who again destroys. Yet, our eyes well up with tears if we look behind. These tears are not of one who is non-materialist or anti-history.

A father organizes a lovely ritual for the marriage of his daughter. He works for re-establishing the girl in her own glory, so that she can start a new life to realize the full potential of her feminine self. Yet, as she stands on the threshold of her new life, he cannot but weep inconsolably for losing the one whom he has reared up with so much care and concern.

The name of Prayag is connected with thousand years of our history. I could not but wonder that the wide avenue on which I was riding a rickshaw today was once part of a dreadful forest, through which Ram, the exiled son of King Dasarath, walked on foot, along with brother Lakshman and wife Sita. He saw a thick smoke curling up from the distant ashram of Sage Bharadwaj. Our myths, legends, epics—all are woven around their story. And also our history.

Suddenly, someone called out, 'Hey, Bengali *bhaiya*!' Along with this address, there were a fountain spring of laughter mixed with the sound of horses' hooves on the pavement and the 'jhum-jhum' of the anklets tied around its neck.

I was lost in the lore of the Ramayana. I woke up as if from a dream and saw Shyama, seated at the base of a tonga, with her feet hanging merrily. In the narrow space within the tonga, the whole family had managed to cram with the old man at the centre. Their tonga was running dangerously close to my rickshaw.

There were more rickshaws and tongas in front, back and sides. Pedestrians were also rushing on both sides of the road. Rows of sadhus were also walking rhythmically. The tinkling sound of the bells of the rickshaws had created a strange music all around.

Shyama was laughing; others in her party were also laughing. Did I see the old man also laughing, or I imagined it? Anyway, there was a hint of pleasantness on the both sides of his nose.

The middle-aged women told Shyama something. In turn, she raised her voice above the cacophany and asked, '*Kahan jana hai*? Where are you going?'

I replied, 'Mela. Kumbh-mela.'

'*Sach*? Is it true?'

There was a hush for a few moments. Perhaps, they had heard something incredible. Then, there was that unbounded stream of spontaneous laughter again. The wayfarers were startled by that laughter; the animals were also surprised by that laughter. Perhaps, for a moment, the endless movement of the human sea stopped at this laughter; perhaps, the moving clouds over Allahabad in the crimson sky of the setting sun paused for a moment at this laughter; perhaps, the chilling wind of the north stopped for a moment at this laughter.

But why so much laughter? In the case of Balaram, I felt that laughter was his life, his song, the apparel of his body. Was it so for these people too? But Balaram's silent laughter opened up life's closed doors. Though silent, it was as if a rousing call for the salvation of humankind. And in the waves of this loud laughter, one could feel the restlessness of the unexpressed agony of a trapped prisoner.

The wheel of my rickshaw was grazing Shyama's hanging feet. It moved away the moment it was about to touch. It was as if Shyama was playing a game. With whom? Me or the rickshawala?

I was under the impression that it was only the Bengali girls who coloured the border of their feet with *alta*, the lac dye. But Shyama's feet were also coloured with the blood-red *alta*.

The feet were partly covered by slippers decorated with butterflies. To boot, there were round and heavy bangles on her ankles. She was wearing a peacock-printed sari, as if a bunch of peacocks were dancing on her power-packed body. Her dry and dust-filled hair was flowing in the wind; a vermillion mark was shining on the parting of her hair. With her two hands adorned with heavily ornate gold bangles, she was holding on her lap a brass pitcher. She was sitting with her neck held high, a bright smile playing out on her lips.

She again asked, 'In which ashram are you putting up?'

I replied, 'I don't know.'

'You don't know?' They exchanged this information among themselves and again started giggling. But how would I know? I have never been to Allahabad, nor have I thought out my plan. What I had thought when I stepped out on the road had become hazy now. But one thing was certain. Despite heavy odds, I was not feeling out of sorts.

In fact, I was desperate to take to the road. Now that restlessness was gone, but my mind had gone crazy. I did not know if my outward appearance had also taken a nutty look. Now, I was intoxicated with the feeling of *charaibati*, 'keep going'. If I kept my ears on my mind, I could only hear, 'Go, go, go!' Thousands of people were going, incessantly. I had also become a drop of water in the moving flood. I did not know where I would finally land up. Who would think of shelter in such a situation where the whole of humanity was moving?

The flow on the road consisted of Punjab, Sind, Bombay, Gujarat, Dravid, Utkal, Bengal. What a variety of appearance! If here was colourful kurta-pajama and *odhni* with braided hair, then there was also multicoloured silk sari-blouse with the chignon adorned by lovely flowers. The upright Sikh was moving with a sheathed knife, hanging from a belt across his chest and a long sword dangling from his waistband. The Delhi woman was making moves in a *ghagra* with a thousand pleats. The Rajput woman was moving with a totally unselfconscious body covered in a fourteen-metre sari of a hundred colours. There was a gold tiara on her forehead and golden bangles and anklets on her hands and feet. Some women were decked in six-inch long heavy nose-rings, some in silver crescent necklaces, some had nose-pins on both sides of the nose and a rosy dot, *bindiya*, on the forehead. The sleek-haired, lungi-clad men were moving with burning cigarettes on their lips. Somewhere, you saw Lucknavi churidar-pyjama; somewhere, well-designed nagra chappals; and somewhere, dhoti-and-loose-kurta-clad Hindustani men with well-groomed moustaches. In the midst of this human procession, one could also find Bengali women clad in handloom saris with designed borders and bright vermillion marks shining on their foreheads. You would also find hapless Bengali widows, in stark white saris, out in search of some solace. And of course, there were dhoti-punjabi-clad Bengali middle-class men like me.

In this procession, the poor India was there like a faded cloth by the side of a muslin chunni. They were moving with worn out blankets, dirty cloths, unkempt hair and pale faces. They were carrying their bundles on their heads. Some had come from the neighbouring villages in bullock carts, some were riding in tongas, some walking. This richness of India is like gold covered in ashes. I wanted to pluck this treasure with both hands.

Observing this great variety of humankind on the move is a thirst that is not easily quenched. I wondered, if the external appearance showed so much variety, how interestingly different would their characters and inner thoughts be. How would I get to know them? My mind turned heavy. Had I not left home to discover the Formless among these forms? Yes, I would dive deep into that heart of India. I would identify my own face in this strange mirror of India. That face is my mind. My religion.

Move on, move on, but how far? How many miles more?

There was an uproar all around. The rattling sound of motor cars, the sound of horses' hooves, the tinkling ankle-bells, the horns of rickshaws. Groups of women walking on the road had started singing in a chorus. If there was song here, there was laughter there, there were crying somewhere else, and there were quarrels still somewhere else. I did not understand everyone's language, nor could I exactly divine the drift of the happenstance.

In this cacophony, suddenly someone shouted out anxiously in rustic Bengali, 'Hey Nidhiram! My dear Nidhiram! Where are you? I have strayed, my son. Hold my hand and pull me to you.'

From some distance, the reply floated in a tired heavy voice, 'Here, *pishi* (aunt), don't get scared. I am not far. I can see you. You won't get lost. Keep moving.'

There is no fear. Keep moving. Who was he talking about? I was confused.

Although I did not understand the meaning of many songs being sung around, my mind lifted up when I heard the strain of a kirtan being sung in accompaniment of drums and cymbals: 'Srikrishna Chaitanya Prabhu Nityananda / Hare Krishna Hare Ram Radhey Gobinda.'

Immediately, Balaram's face flashed across my mind. Who was singing this song? Was it Lakshmidasi's group?

A road sign said it was Kamala Nehru Road. The corporation-women were sweeping the ungravelled parts on both sides of the road. They had tied their brooms on top of bamboo sticks, so that they could sweep without bending. While doing so, they were looking at the mela-going pilgrims with wide wonder. There was not even a single drop of water. I did not understand why they were raising additional dust by sweeping the dry road.

We, the Kumbh-goers, were using today a path steeped in history. We could find the dust of Gautam Buddha's lotus feet on this road. If we put our ears on this road, we could hear the victorious march of the Mauryan Army. We could see the deeply enchanted Greek Ambassador Megasthenes or the Chinese traveller Fa-hien. We could hear the rattling sound of the wheels of the chariots of Samudragupta and Harshavardhan. We could detect the footprints of Hiuen Tsang and Shankaracharya.

But that history is of Prayag, not of Allahabad. According to researchers, Prayag was once called Vatsadesh; its capital, Kaushambi, was on the bank of the river, Yamuna. Then the formidable Mughal Army overran it. The great Mughal emperor came to Prayag and re-christened it as Illahabas. He laid the foundation of the Illahabas fort. Gradually, this Illahabas turned into a favourite pasture for the succeeding emperors. Jahangir built his favourite Khasrubag. Shahjahan renamed the city Illahabad.

After that also, Illahabad suffered the aggression of ruthless Bundela rebels and dauntless Maratha cavalry. The soil of Illahabad was soaked with the blood of fallen soldiers. At times, the canons of the Mughals occupied it, at other times, the swords of the Marathas.

Then there was total darkness. The debt-ridden Nawab of Oudh sold her to the East India Company.

Today we are marching on her. We are not historical travellers, but history is being created in our mind.

A sudden jolt almost threw me out of my rickshaw. I managed to support myself by leaning my weight on a heavy utensil. It was Shyama's pitcher. The traffic police had suddenly raised his hand. As a result, the whole procession of mobile carriages had come to a screeching halt.

I removed my hand quickly. Shyama was giggling in open amusement.

'I was a little unmindful,' I said defensively.

Shyama looked at me with teasing eyes and said, 'Thinking of people at home, I suppose?'

More laughter. Strange! Is laughter an ailment for her?

The elder woman of the group asked, 'What happened?'

Shyama threw me a sidelong glance and smoothly replied with silent laughter, 'Nothing. The Bengali brother saved my pitcher from falling.'

I looked at Shyama in amazement. But she was examining my face with such searching looks that I almost blushed and quickly averted her eyes.

Normally, there was no scope of feeling embarrassed in a journey. After all, the acquaintances on the road would end with the road. I did not know how coquettish Shyama was, what secret play of emotion was there in her unabashed nimbleness. Taking her secret games within herself, she would go in one direction and I would go in another. So, who cares?

But the question of public embarrassment was there. There were people in front, people behind. Everybody was looking, everybody was listening. It was one thing to laugh out, it was another thing to keep staring with mischievous laughter.

'Why are you looking at me like this?' I asked.

She brushed the flowing hair back from her face and replied in a teasing low tone, 'I am not looking. It is you who is looking.'

Well, she had me there. Yes, I had looked at her many times since morning. It was not a pre-meditated action. It was impossible not to look at her. Who does not look at the sky when walking in the open? Who does not look at the flowers when crossing a garden? Who can avoid looking at the singing bird somersaulting in the sky? Shyama was a natural looker like that. Moreover, I had stepped out on the road to see everything and everyone.

But I had asked something in one tone, got a reply in a different tone. And the reply was peppered with accusation. I had no other way but to concede defeat. In such matters, we always concede defeat to the Shyamas of the world.

Finding me silent, Shyama was more amused. Bending down a little, she again asked, 'Tell me, what were you looking at?'

This time I played along. 'It is you only. Your lac dye-smeared feet, your peacock-printed sari….'

Shyama quickly averted her face. So, the mysterious woman had to fake unmindfulness even at this light flattery! Was she feeling shy? Or was she repenting that she had given a stranger too much indulgence?

But Shyama was quick to recover. She turned around as if she had not heard my earlier comment and said ruefully, 'My throat is still hurting. If you had put a little more pressure in that crowded compartment, I would have perhaps died.'

So she was trying to change the drift of the conversation. Yet the hint of mischief did not totally leave her face when she asked, 'Why were you carrying that Bengali lame *sadhu* on your back? *Koi jaan-pahechan*, someone known to you?'

'No.'

'Then why?'

I said, 'You hung on the elbow of a timid man like me. Are you someone known to me, *koi jaan-pahechan*?'

A lightning of surprise flashed across Shyama's face. Then she tittered sweetly and said, '*Ajeeb admi*! Strange person!'

The traffic police had given the go-ahead signal. The procession started moving again. In one jerky movement, Shyama's tonga moved quite ahead of us. I could not hear the comment Shyama made that led to a huge guffaw of laughter from the group of women.

As we moved on, I noticed a road sign across the long North–South road reading Grand Trunk Road. We were moving from the east to the west, albeit in slight angular movement. Among the clamouring of the human sea, one could hear the familiar stale songs blaring out of the microphone.

Looking forward, I could see a vast field with endless rows of tents and sheds. Was this the mela? It was looking like a horizon-less ocean with waves of tents and temporary sheds. But what a nuisance! Here too, the sweeper-women were as if celebrating Holi with dust. The vast expanse of arid land was totally barren, there was not even a shred of grass. It was all covered with dust. I failed to understand what order had been issued by the civic authorities to keep it clean. And what pleasure the sweepers were deriving by working up a storm of dust. Was there no drop of water in this land?

Dusk was falling. But there was premature darkness because of the dust. Forget the men and women, even the horses started snorting. Many people were riding on donkeys. They also started braying. To confound the confusion, all the tongas, rickshaws and other vehicles started moving down from the road to that dust-laden tract of land.

Alarmed, I asked the rickshaw-puller, 'Where are you going?'

He replied, 'Babu, all vehicles are supposed to stop here. Then, we are to buy tickets for going up to the embankment. Give me six annas for that.'

'You have wrangled two rupees out of me for this distance deserving eight annas. Now, you are asking for six annas more?'

With his sweat-drenched, dirty face, the rickshaw-puller gave me a broad smile and said, 'Rule, Babusaheb. Unless you buy ticket, the rickshaw will not be allowed to go any farther.'

He looked around and parked his rickshaw near a tonga. Hearing familiar snatches of laughter, I could gauge in the dusky haze that the tonga belonged to Shyama and Co. My rickshawalla seemed to have a sharp eye. But I was not going to give him any extra *baksish* for this.

Handing over six annas to him, I instructed. 'Come back quickly.'

Then I pulled out my handkerchief and pressed it over my face and nose. I was feeling stifled due to the dust.

Someone commented from nearby, 'Oh, the wretched fellow!'

I could barely open my eyes because of the dust, but Shyama and another of her friends were undaunted. They were looking at me with mock sympathy. Behind their faces, I could see the burning eyes of the old man. He was staring at me like a provoked tiger. One could not blame him. As a guardian, how long could he stand this frivoulous conversation?

I asked Shyama, 'Is the old man your father?'

'Father! Tut, tut, why should he be my father?'

Was the reaction a bit too sharp? I could not see clearly, but it seemed Shyama smiled in embarrassment and turned around her face.

I asked, 'Then who is he?'

There was no reply. I looked hard and was surprised too see that Shyama was looking vacantly far straight ahead. There was an unexpected gravity in her face. Were my eyes playing trick with me in this dust storm? Or was the shadow across her face real? Perhaps, I should not have pressed it any further, but I could not suppress my curiosity and pushed on, 'You didn't reply to my question.'

Then a sardonic smile flashed across Shyama's face, like a lightning in the darkness, as she replied, 'My husband.'

Husband? This octogenarian old man? Was it also one of Shyama's pranks? But I dared not repeat the question.

Rather, I gestured at the elderly woman and asked, 'She?'

With the same smile, Shyama replied. 'My co-wife.'

'And the other two?'

'One is my step-sister's sister and the other is a servant.'

A number of questions rushed to my lips, but I held the rein and just asked, 'What is your caste?'

Shyama replied, 'Bhuihar.'

I had heard about the Bhuihars. They were caste-Hindus like the Brahmins and the Kayasthas. It is said that their *kuleen* system was very strict and rigorous.

If a matching groom was not available, girls had to remain as spinsters at their parent's homes. For a Bengali, this was not news. A lot of Bengali girls have sacrificed their happiness as victims of *kuleen* system.

But Shyama was not so old that she had to be married to a doddering old man whose skin hangs loose. I had heard that the Bhuihars were generally quite well-to-do. Perhaps the consolation lay there.

I dared not look at Shyama anymore. I had known her for a very short time. As I was not a religious pilgrim, she must have taken me for a *musafir*—a traveller. We did not know each other's lifestyle. Travelling companionship just resulted in some kind of bonding. And for a girl like Shyama, it does not take long to break the barrier of unfamiliarity.

Still, I could not muster courage to look at her. The lightning-like flashes of smile on her lips were enough to singe the heart of the entire male community. When the lightning of the sky strikes down as thunder, it revels in death and devastation.

In a hushed but intense voice, Shyama quipped, 'So, you have no more questions?' Posing this playful query, she burst out in a peel of laughter.

But that laughter did not move me anymore. I realized that what I construed as the ear-splitting vigorous sound of an advancing wild horse, was that of a mere tame circus horse. Its movement is determined by the whip of the ringmaster.

Hearing her laughter, the elderly woman again asked, 'What's the matter, Shyama?'

Immediately Shyama changed her demeanour. With a smirk on her lips, she replied in a disapproving tone, 'Look at this man, asking me a hundred questions: Who is he? Who is she? What is your caste? Why Mister, how does all this concern you?'

Everyone laughed out in chorus. As if Shyama suddenly turned coy like an ordinary village maiden, as if she was trying to take revenge on me for some imagined crime that I have committed.

Although I was supposed to be embarrassed, I was not. Shyama's sudden transformation did not touch me at all. I could see that Shyama's contempt was not towards me, but towards herself and the whole society. She had suffered indignity by expressing herself before me in an unguarded moment. Perhaps, she tried to fortify herself against that self-inflicted insult.

She might have said something more. But the tongawala came back with tickets and her tonga started moving. I wished with all my heart that she would leave the poison in her mind with me and move on to dip in the pitcher of nectar. I waited all ears to hear the parting laughter. Shyama was looking in this direction. The moment her tonga started to move, the contemptuous smirk vanished from her lips. There was no animosity, no joy, no smile. It was an expressionless face, her vacant gaze was at the horizon. That bright light was gone from her eyes, as if she had gone blind. Only the two eyes of the old man blazed from behind her.

I was almost blinded by the dust. Even my mouth was making a grating noise as if I was chewing dust. But this was just as it should be. When I hit the road, I was playing the *ektara* of my mind in a particular tune. Who guaranteed that there would be continuous joy? It was expected that at times, the strain would go out of tune.

After a few moments, the rickshaw-puller returned with tickets and my rickshaw also left the dusty field and climbed up to the road. On both sides of the way to the embankment, petty traders had set up temporary shops. Lights were coming up in them. Noise was increasing gradually.

By then, I was tired to the bone. My eyes were heavy with sleep. The rickshaw stopped. We had reached the destination. The dyke was in front of us. We needed to cross it and go to the other side. Paying off the rickshaw, I climbed upon the dam and stood for a few moments. The Ganga was flowing nearby from north to south. Its current was fast. The bank of the river was brightly lit for the mela.

On the other side, one could see the sea of tents in the light and shade. The vast stretch of land beyond the tents was covered in the haze of dusk. On the eastern side, there was a slightly elevated ground where a village stood surrounded by trees and plants. Maybe, the well dug by Samudragupta lay somewhere there on a hillock. On the far south, I could faintly see the trace of a running water like a silver foil.

So, this is Prayag—'Pra' (brief form of *prakrishta*, meaning the best) + 'yag' (corrupt form of yajna, meaning sacrificial ritual). According to the ancient Puranas, this place was at the centre of Lord Brahma's *yajna* altar. The history of religion in ancient India played out here. The smoke from the first rituals of yajna in this world spread over the sky above this place. Prayag is that holy land:

Sitasitey saritey yatra sangatey
Tatrahalpa taso divamutpatanti.
Ye boi tanung visrijanti dhirah
Te boi janasohamritatwang bhajantey.

So be it. But I was a householder who had stepped out on the road. I needed a shelter. I had not booked a place in advance, so I would have to search for one. But where would I look for accommodation under this open sky, amid this sea of tents? The mind might be vagrant, the heart might be a renunciator, but the body was already stiffening under the biting cold. Lack of cover might lead to imminent death on the road like a real vagabond!

I quickly ran down the embankment to look for a shelter. The atmosphere all around was gorgeous, but I did not have the mental condition to appreciate it. There were people in front of me, there were people behind me, there were people on my left, there were people on my right. All were not moving in the same direction. The crowd was moving helter-skelter. Were they all looking for shelter? With my bags and baggages, I would collide with one on the left and then one on the right. From the movement of the crowd, I guessed that the destination lay on the other side of the Ganga.

There was a floating bridge to cross the river. I have heard that such bridges are extremely necessary in modern warfare. Nearby, one could see the camp of the army and the PWD. The uniformed army personnels were controlling the traffic on the bridge. Rows of light were coming up on the bridge. Their reflections on the river were broken up in fragments because of the strong current.

But what would I gain by crossing the river? In the light fog on the other side, I could see a thousand lights burning and hundreds of grey tents standing. Hundreds of people were coming, hundreds of people were going. On both sides of the river, the air was reverberating with the sound of hymns, mantras, bhajans and kirtans coming out of the amplifiers. Coupled with it, there was the noise of thousands of confused pilgrims.

My mind had turned crazy for stepping out. But now I could not perhaps stand like a mad fellow for ever. Suddenly, I spotted a vendor selling food stuff under a banyan tree. Good God! The mendicant soul, which was happy with just tea throughout the day, suddenly cried out for food. There was no piety in empty stomach. My hungry eyes were immediately glued to the signboards disclaiming *desi gheeun ki puri* (hand-bread made with home-made ghee), *doodh ke malai* (cream of milk), laddoo, sandesh and more. I was aware that open food stuff in such a fair were sure recipe for cholera; still my tongue started salivating at the prospect of tasting some.

Before I could make up my mind, the constant thrust of the crowd pushed me away from the spot. Suddenly, I noticed a signboard on the entrance of a camp, declaring 'Enquiry'. I decided to try my luck there.

Before starting for this journey, I had thought that Prayag being one of the major pilgrimages, a shelter would automatically work out. There is a saying that you can come out of the clutches of Yama, but not that of a panda. Not that I did not have any prior experience of this.

A few years back, I had to visit Puri. Not during the peak season. It was an untimely call. I had heard that during tourist seasons, people from various walks of life—right from Bhutos-Gadais-Puntis from Bongaon to the city-bred Swapnas-Shipras-Shubhras to the *awara* gang to pen-pushing clerk to the professor with oratorial skill to the writer with magical pen and the seasoned scholars—all used to blossom like seasonal flowers on the beaches of Puri.

However, I did not have such luck. During my trip, the sky was replete with thunder clouds and the ocean was spewing waves of fury.

But that is a different story. As I reached the Puri railway station, pandas pounced upon the passengers like scourge. As if a regiment of hungry lions had been set upon a bunch of unsuspecting people. They totally outnumbered the passengers and vied with each other to capture the pilgrims. As a lone luggage-less passenger, I managed to dodge the pandas and came out of the station. But as I climbed upon a cycle-rickshaw, an old fellow materialized from nowhere, jumped into the running rickshaw and took a seat by me. When I angrily accosted him, he laughed merrily and introduced himself. I realized that he was a panda. I also learnt that his ancestors had served as priests for many aristocratic families of Bengal. Hence, I had no other alternative but to be his guest.

Though I managed to survive his terribly slippery and dirty washing space around a well, I almost cried when food was served. Rice-gruel mixed with turmeric powder was being passed for dal and arum fry as potato fry. The panda and his wife were making sweet-talk as a part of hospitality, and a bride with a nose ring and thick lips was serving the food. Under normal circumstances, the scene could pass for a typical Bengali hospitality, complete with insistence for taking a little bit more. But here, the trap was only to swindle money out of the unwary pilgrim. I ran away from these thugs paying through my nose. The sea beach of Puri though was a welcome relief, a balmy breath for my arum-burning throat.

But I am digressing. In fact, I cannot help telling a story if there is one to be told. It is like an addiction. What I wanted to say is that the scourge of the panda was totally absent in Prayag. If it were there, I would have got a shelter by now, good or bad.

On entering the enquiry camp, I found an officer writing something on his desk while a sepoy was standing in attention. I began to say, 'Excuse me…'

The officer's pen stopped moving. He gave me a searching look from top to bottom and said, '*Aap photo khichney mangta hai*—you want to take photographs? I am sorry, photography is strictly prohibited in the fare.'

I was completely taken aback. Did I look like a photographer? The overcoat I was carrying was covered with dust. I had two *jhola*s hanging from my shoulders. There was not even a camera in my hand. How did the question of photography come up?

I said, 'No, no, I am not talking about photography. Could you tell me where I can find a place to stay here?'

Now, the officer looked surprised. He said, 'Why, you can stay wherever you like. In an *ashram*, in the camp of the pandas. Alternatively, you can construct your own shanty by using leaves and bamboos. Where do you come from?'

'Calcutta.'

The officer thought for a moment and said, 'It may be wiser for you to try a room at Ramakrishna Mission or Bharat Sevashram Sangh.'

Without explaining why it would be wiser for me, he went back to his work. But I had to ask again, 'Can you please tell me the direction to Bharat Sevashram Sangh? For that matter, Ramakrishna Mission too?'

Without raising his head, he gave a brief reply, 'One is on the other side of the embankment and the other is on the other side of the Ganga.'

Then he started giving some fast instruction to the sepoy. I realized that my enquiry time was over. As I came out of the camp, a gust of cold hit me like a whiplash. I quickly put down the *jhola*s and put on the overcoat.

After dusk, the dust and smoke had engulfed the entire area. Though there was light, the people moving around were looking like shadows. As if under the open sky of the Sangam, a mysterious scene was being enacted in diffused light, on a stage.

I wondered if all this was a hallucination of my hungry and exhausted brain. There was so much of crowd, so much of noise around me and yet it all seemed very far.

Suddenly, my mind started thinking in a reverse manner. Nah, I would not go hunting for a shelter. I thought that I had come to see all this. Then, why remain confined to a room? I did not know how such a thought occurred to me. Was it from disgust, from a sense of frustration? Was it the feeling of some anguish or some kind of masochism—a desire to punish myself?

A strange thought occurred to me. I had left the struggle for survival behind in the city of Calcutta; then why should I run hither and thither for the same struggle here in Kumbh? Why not spend the night on this sand-band itself?

While indulging in such wild speculations, I was suddenly jolted to attention by a raucous voice. Whose voice was it? Something familiar in it immediately made me shake off my stupor and give a searching look through the haze of smog. Though I could not see anything, I again heard that coarse and shrill voice speaking in rustic Bengali, 'Don't give me any more trouble, Pellad. This time, I will drown myself in the Ganga, you'll see.'

In reply, Prahlad's rude voice was heard. 'Do whatever you like. If I don't go away with my wife tomorrow, then—'

'I warn you, Pellad. Don't swear in a divine place.'

'I'll swear. I'll swear a thousand times. Let me see who can stop me.'

'Well, then go ahead and swear. You will also see how I jump into the river, Ganga.'

But Prahlad was unrelenting, 'I would surely swear. I don't care if you jump into the river. Gosh, throughout my whole life, I have not allowed any syringe to push inside me. Now, I had to take injection here, along with my wife, thanks to your stinginess. Now if something happens to me...'

'But have they exempted this old woman, you moron?'

This time, a grave voice admonished them, 'Shut up, you two. How long will you continue this tirade?'

I cannot tell you how this old drama rejuvenated me. Didima and Prahlad's voices might be grating and coarse, but they sounded very sweet to me. They were like straws for a drowning man. All my frustration, all my anguish was gone. Here were some old acquaintances; why should not I go with them? Why should I spend a restless night in this horrible expanse of sand?

There I could see Prahlad pushing ahead in the crowd, holding Didima in one hand and his wife in the other, his old shawl loosely hanging from his body. I surged ahead of the crowd and reached them. It is Didima who noticed me first. Pat came the expected response, 'There you are! You don't have to show me all your teeth in an attempt to smile.'

I immediately shut my mouth. True, I had taken the injection first and in a way pushed them into it. The crime was mine.

Prahlad said, 'There you are, Sir. The bastards did not spare us after all. Pushed the syringe in.' He changed the voice the next moment and complained, 'What terrible pain! I am sure I have a bout of fever coming.'

Didima's reaction was sharp, 'Again inauspicious words and thoughts! You don't have fever at all.'

'I say I have fever. Now, if something happens to me—'

Suddenly Didima started whimpering. Trying to keep in check the tears rushing into her eyes, she uttered in a muffled voice, 'O God, let his statement be false. I have come so far in search of you. How can you send fever to my Pellad?'

Perhaps, Prahlad had also got wind of Didima's silent prayer. He kept blabbering for my benefit. 'You know, this old hag is so stingy. I have to toil very hard just to extricate two annas from her everyday.'

I got curious, 'Why two annas everyday?'

He laughed conspiratorially, which sounded like a hiccup and said, 'Don't ask me. I am getting fed up. For the last two days, my chest is "starving". Gosh, who would have agreed to come here, if it was known in advance?'

Noticing my blank look, Prahlad leaned forward and said in a lower tone, 'No, you are hopeless. Come on, I mean the *prasad* of Lord Shiva.'

'You mean hemp?'

Prahlad bit his tongue and replied, 'Don't call it hemp. It's Lord Shiva's grace.'

I heard Didima's sharp reaction, 'Fie on this ganja-smoker! Even on a pilgrimage, he keeps thinking of his own addiction… Now, hello Panch-Baidya, my legs are giving away. How far, my son?'

The man in front turned around for the first time. Why this mountain of a man was called Panch-Baidya was something I could not make out. But I shuddered to look at his face. As if somebody had hammered at it with extreme cruelty. The head was disproportionately long, the forehead was swelled forward, the eyes were protruding from deep sockets. Add flat nose and thick lips to these, and he made quite a spectacle. Even in this biting cold, he was wearing just a pair of trousers and a bush shirt. And yet he was walking straight, without bending forward even an inch.

He replied, 'We have to cross the bridge and walk a little farther.' Having said so, he stared at me with disapproving eyes.

We were stopped at the bridge by a sentry who declared, 'This is a one-way bridge for coming from the other side. For going to the other side you will have to use the southern bridge.'

So we did. There was pandemonium at the mouth of the bridge. Those who had come on rickshaws and tongas were all alighting at that point. No carrier was allowed to climb upon the bridge. It was only for walking across. Hence, there was a jostling crowd and a cacophony of noises.

It was a pontoon bridge. Under the pressure of human weight, it was making croaking sounds. Water was also swelling up under this pressure. The ever-flowing river, Ganga, was moving with strong current.

On the other side of the river, the temperature felt to be a notch further down. Just below the bridge, a row of people sat with lighted lamps. They were shouting, '*Gheeun ki diya*! (ghee-lamps), just four paisa a piece. Pay your homage to the Mother Ganga, babu.'

I saw a number of such lamps floating on the river. Their reflections on the water made their number look double. I had no idea how Mother Ganga was receiving these lamps. What I could see was a bunch of naked boys jumping in the river and carefully guiding the lamps towards a particular direction. Maybe towards their home. For recycling? Or was it just for fun?

I was walking like an intoxicated person, side-stepping the entrances of various tents. The soles of my feet were digging into the merciless cold sand. At places, the mendicant monks had sat down on the sand, putting fire on incensory.

Prahlad called out, 'Doctor-uncle.'

I realized that the Frankenstein-looking fellow was also a doctor. His serious look made it quite plausible.

Panch-Baidya replied, 'Yes.'

'How far from here?'

'Almost there. See those lights on the southeast? That is our ashram.'

Prahlad said happily, 'Wow! The ashram looks great. Are there songs playing on the mike too, uncle?'

He responded self-congratulatingly, 'Yes, dear. You know, Khurhi, I have booked ourselves in such an ashram that you would feel you are staying at your home.'

So, Prahlad's Didima was his *khurhi*, paternal aunt. She responded with gratitude, 'You are a dear. Without you we could not have come here. For me, who else is there apart from you?'

Was there a subtle jibe at Prahlad? But Prahlad did not seem to take note of it.

The old lady was panting. Perhaps, Prahlad's wife also was short of breath. She was a chit of a girl, not more than thirteen or fourteen. This long walk and the terrible cold had got the better of her. She had virtually given herself up on Prahlad's shoulder and was staggering along blindly.

Without turning around, Panch-Baidya asked, 'Khurhi, who is this fellow?'

Didima looked at me and replied, 'I have no idea, son.'

Panch-Baidya turned towards me and asked roughly, 'Where are you going?'

I mumbled, 'Well, I am looking for a shelter.'

This time, he barked out the question, 'But why are you tagging along with us?'

I almost stopped in my track at the nature of reception, 'I just need a place at least for the night.'

Panch-Baidya warned in a grave tone, 'I have seen enough of such street-smartness. Now get lost.'

I looked at Prahlad for some support. Prahlad smiled and said, 'You were doing fine, but now there is an obstacle. Better to part ways.'

Didima took a different route. In an indignant tone she chastised me, 'It is good that you are travelling light, but couldn't you have arranged a place for stay in advance?'

A justified accusation. I had not come here with grandma's passionate devotion to God. I had not come here to earn piety. Nor had I come here to complete a circle of pilgrimage. So, it is I who should have made all material arrangements in advance. But unfortunately, things had happened the opposite here.

Didima softened her coarse voice as much as possible and told Panch-Baidya, 'Look, Panchugopal, this boy is from our own land, Bengal. People say, one should not drive away even cats and dogs in a pilgrimage. Will it be proper to drive the boy away?'

Panch-Baidya retorted angrily, 'You won't understand these tricks, Khurhi. This is Kumbh-mela, you know. Even a sleeping man gets abducted here. What if this fellow slips away with our belongings at night?'

The statement was insulting. But objections to it would be futile. By that time, we had reached the ashram's gate. It was a large fenced space with a raised platform in the middle with a deity mounted on it, and about ten tents for the pilgrims. A few saffron-clad sadhus were singing, sitting in front of microphones on the platform. There was a wooden throne, on which was seated a sadhu with matted hair and his whole body covered in ash. A few hundred men and women were sitting around and listening to the songs.

Didima bowed her forehead down on the threshold at the entrance of the ashram. Standing up, she hesitated for a moment and then said, 'Panchu, let the boy also come in. Where will he go at this time of the night?'

'Let him go wherever he wishes to. Why do you care, aunt? Where will he stay here?'

Saying so, Panch-Baidya moved forward. Didima shook her mop of dry grey hair and told me, 'Come, come over. All troubles are for me to take care.'

Somehow, I found this soft assurance from a coarse voice more powerful than the menacing warning of Panch-Baidya. Who ever imagined that the old hag of Allahabad station would appear as a saviour for me here? I felt like touching her feet right then and there, but had to check my emotion, because I was still apprehensive of the final outcome.

This time, however, Prahlad also added, 'Come on, sir. The doctor-uncle always talks like that. Slightly off his hook, you know.'

I did not know who was off his hook here, but I tagged along. A few feet forward and Panch-Baidya reappeared with a sadhu who must have been a Vaishnava. There was a long line of sandalwood paste drawn from the tip of his nose to the top of his forehead. With his saffron cloth and the tuft of hair adorning his head, he looked like the Adhyaksha—the Director of the ashram. With folded hands, he told me, 'We don't have any tent for an unaccompanied man. If you had come with your family, I could have perhaps arranged some accommodation for you. Here, people are staying with their wives, mothers and daughters. How can we accommodate a single male?'

But my shelter was at Didima's heart. Before I could reason with the Adhyaksha, Didima raised her voice a notch higher and said indignantly, 'This is unfair, Panchu. How could you describe the boy as a single male visitor?' Then turning to the Adhyaksha, she declared, 'He has come with us. He will stay in our tent. If he misbehaves with any female around, you can drive all of us out.'

Panch-Baidya's ungainly face registered extreme embarrassment. The sadhu was also greatly surprised. I was totally bowled out. I never thought that Didima would go to that extent.

Prahlad piped in, 'Yes, sadhu-baba. Doesn't he look like a better gentleman than us? If you cannot accommodate him, then throw us out too.'

The sadhu quickly retraced his steps, 'Oh no, if he stays with you, we have no objection.'

Then, he turned towards me and said, 'You please make arrangements with them. I was only citing general rules of the ashram. No offence intended.'

Once he left, Panchu sullenly addressed Didima and said, 'Come, let me show you your tent.'

One tent had been divided into two halves, each half accommodating one family. Paddy-straw had been spread over the floor for the comfort of sitting and sleeping. However, there was electric light as a small mercy. Yes, the arrangement was as good as your home!

Although I was quite embarrassed for this gate-crashing, I entered the tent with Didima and got rid of my bag and baggage first. Then I flopped on the cushion of hay in sheer fatigue.

Everyone was in the same condition. Only Panch-Baidya was shouting in disgust, 'It was a blunder on my part to bring you people. Had I known earlier that an unwanted fellow would tag along, I would have never taken this responsibility. But look here, young fellow—'

He was addressing me. I kept looking at him. Panch-Baidya made a combative gesture of thumping at his chest and declared, 'My name is Dr Panchugopal Ray. If you indulge in the slightest act of transgression, I will break your neck. Stay just for the night. Tomorrow, I will take care of you.'

After he left, I kept sitting like a scared boy. Time is the ultimate tyrant. Today was his time. In future, time would come for me to give a befitting reply to Panch-Baidya. For the present, I was poison for him. Didima had absorbed that poison in her breast.

Looking around, I found Didima busy in organizing her homestead with the help of her granddaughter-in-law. I was quite oblivious to what they were chattering about. I was thinking that it was futile to look for the real person in his or her external appearance. One had to dive deep in his or her heart. My body was fatigued and famished. Yet, my eyes welled up with tears. Perhaps, I hit the road to see this internal beauty of mankind. Curiously, I was discovering it in my insult, in my helplessness and in my tears.

Feeling extremely thirsty, I went out in search of some water. Behind our tent, I found a water-tap, but there was a long queue of men and women. Some were washing dishes, others doing some kind of ablutions.

Somebody said loudly, 'Binu, you are an idiot. You have burnt the entire curry.' In response, someone giggled with the sound of a cascading fountain. Perhaps, Binu herself.

Someone chastised someone else, 'Enough. Now move away with your utensils. Can't keep waiting for the whole day.'

A woman's voice floated out from the tent near-by, 'Are you talking of Anil's father-in-law? Heard that the bugger is a big shot. That's why Anil's wife has so much vanity.'

Suddenly, I felt as if I had entered into a blind, narrow lane of a gloomy slum in a mufussil town of Bengal. The slum life at dusk. Noise and uproar all around—brawls, loud music, uninvited comments, discussions of humdrum everyday life. Along with all this, the symphony of running tap-water, clattering of utensils and all.

I forgot that I was on a pilgrimage. I was, for all that I could see and hear, standing in an undefined slice of Bengal. My mind felt fresh. The sight of water made me feel even fresher. It was quite a few days that I had had a bath. Today, I must splash water on my body, howsoever cold it might be.

I ducked down to enter the tent again. From the bag, I hunted out my towel and soap. Let me cleanse the body first. We will see about the mind later.

But before I could make a move towards the tent-door, I heard the shrill voice of Didima, or Mother Goddess, 'What a blasphemy is this!'

I turned around to see who it was addressed to and was stunned to find that her large fiery eyes were directed towards me. I immediately shrank in anticipation of another wave of shame and scandal. I barely managed to ask in a broken voice, 'What's wrong?'

Didima raised her voice a pitch higher and said, 'What's wrong, he asks. Well, I condoned the act of taking injection. That was due to fear of death. But on what ground you dare using a soap in a pilgrimage? Don't you know even this much that soap and oil deface the place of God?' I did not know this great homily. Objection was useless. Who knew that the greatness of gods could also be washed away by oil and soap?

But I would never brag my ability to understand human nature. The same person to whom I was bending down in gratitude a few moments earlier was the last whom I would like to engage with now. On the contrary, I was seeking the earliest opportunity to flee from her proximity. Do they express their love and affection as well as anger and repulsion with the same level of intensity?

Prahlad was thoroughly enjoying the bliss of rest. Gazing at me indulgently, he said, 'You know, Didima, the fellow is a thorough-bred gentleman!'

'I bet,' grunted Didima.

This gave me the escape route. I caught hold of the towel and rushed out, leaving the soap behind. After pouring water all over my body, I realized my terrible mistake. The water was bitingly cold. My teeth started chattering and my whole body started shivering like a patient afflicted with malaria. This is one disease we Bengalis specialize in. I may not be able to describe the sharpness of Uttar Pradesh winter, but

I could expertly describe, even show off, the experience of this malaria-proof lean body nurtured in the environment of Bengal. For example, for months together we could tell the time just by watching the moment when body temperature started rising. Is this any less feat? With a belly bloated by a huge spleen, hands and feet like dry twigs and large liquid eyes, we could still look at the azure sky of Bengal in search of poetic inspiration and sing out,

Come, my sporting Radha,
Let's go and dally with Black Pearl (Krishna)
At the market-place of romance.

But the cold was getting unbearable. I forced all this nostalgic thought out of my mind and entered the tent, still shivering. What I saw inside filled my mind with gratitude. Didima was a real chameleon! My bag had been unpacked and one blanket had been spread over the hay. A makeshift pillow had been made with my other bag and the second blanket had been kept folded at the feet of the so-called bed. It was so inviting that I quickly rubbed myself dry, put on the overcoat and stretched in the bed, covering myself head to toe with the other blanket.

The whole Prahlad family along with Didima were staring at me without any word. Now I heard the full-throated phlegm-infused laughter of Didima. Once she had managed to control the laughter a little, she called out, 'Hello, young man. Were you not about to use soap on your body in total disregard of custom? Then what are you so finicky about?'

I queried, 'Finicky?'

'Yes. We have also touched people of different castes on our way, but we have not ventured to bathe in this cold weather.'

It was pointless here to try to convince anyone that I bathed not to save my caste, but to cleanse myself. No one would believe. It was better to avoid any argument. So, I just smiled and turned to the other side.

Didima again declared loudly, 'Look here, don't get yourself a pneumonia, I won't be able to handle it.'

Listen to the power of words. Who was asking whom to handle what? I was supposed to relieve them by leaving in the morning. Then how did the question of her handling my pneumonia arise?

Some arrangement for food was also in the offing. There was no question of cooking so late at night, but some *chnirhe*, flattened rice, and jaggery were being distributed. I felt terribly embarrassed. If I could only stay outside during this dinner time!

The inevitable voice of Didima again, 'Come, eat something before you sleep.'

Though I was so fatigued that I would have preferred sleep to food at that point, I dared not argue with Didima and chewed some *chnirhe* and jaggery before retiring.

Outside in the ashram courtyard, divine discourses over the microphone were still going on. In fact, throughout the Kumbh-mela, huge din and bustle could still be heard in full flow. I could also hear low conversations in the nearby tents. But I felt as if I was far from all these happenings.

As I was floating in and out of sleep, suddenly my ears caught the lilting snatches of a song:

Sri Nanda baptised him son of Nanda,
Yashoda called him, my loving Jadu...

It was Didima's drowsy voice. But it whipped up my ear drum with a jerk. From the ear drum, a strange thrill ran through my body.

It was the hundred and eight names of Lord Krishna. I could never commit it to memory. Nor did I realize the glory of these names. But during my childhood, this song sung in a muffled voice would put an end to all my pranks, all the dreams of my sleepless eyes and all my global curiosities.

My mother's embrace and this song would run through the veins of my childish body and envelop the entire world of my sleep and dream. Not only would this song lull me into sleep at night, it would also wake me up in the morning.

Then I drifted away in the current of life like a flower torn from its stalk. The youth greeted me with endless struggle and pain. In trying to find my feet on the earth, I did not know when I had lost that tune.

But I was not aware that this lost tune had been unknowingly flowing through my blood for all these years. All the noises died out. Even while gradually lapsing into a deep slumber, I could hear the snatches of the song:

Radha Binodini named him Black Gold
Kubja called him...

At the dead of night, I was jolted awake by a rustling sound. My hay-bed was at the corner of the tent, by the side of the screen. At first, I could not open my eyes. The cold wind from outside was entering the tent through the gap under the screen. My whole body shivered. It felt as if the blood had frozen inside my hands and feet. Perhaps it is this cold wave that had woken me up. The mela was now calm and quiet. One could only hear the sudden toll of an irregular bell. But the rustling sound came again from very near my ears. Opening my eyes, I was startled to see a pair of boots. Gingerly, I looked above the boots to see a pair of coarse khaki pants and then the torso covered by a heavy blanket.

What the hell! It was the monster of the movie 'Frankenstein'—Panch-Baidya. Dr Panchugopal was scanning the inside of the tent with a ferocious face. He could not gauge that I was awake. I did not know what he was looking for. My sole concern was if he would just raise one foot and bring down the boot on my throat!

A few breathless moments. Then I heard his suppressed fury, 'Damn! No place for me to sleep. I have to roam outside.'

Next moment, he raised a corner of the screen and stormed out, letting another gush of biting wind to my discomfiture.

But why was the doctor searching for a shelter in this cold night? I could not comprehend the situation. By that time, sleep had totally deserted me. I have heard that sometimes, excessive fatigue works on our nerves in such a manner that instead of falling fast asleep, you tend to remain awake. But there was no slackness in my mind. On the contrary, it was eager to see more, hear more. Shorn of all lethargy, it was full of curiosity.

I got up and went out, buttoning my overcoat. Immediately, I was almost immobilized by the cold. I have heard that winter in Europe was terrible. Water freezes into ice there. The houses and roads become covered by snow. People feel afraid to go out. But my Bengali bones are crushed by the cold of UP, let alone the UK. I quickly fished out my muffler from the coat-pocket and covered my head securely. The lights on the outer side of the ashram had been switched off. Just behind the podium, a makeshift temple had been built with thatches of fanpalm leaves. Its doors were now closed, but a few people were sleeping on the podium and below it, totally covered with blankets. They were looking like bundles thrown down here and there.

I went out of the main gate of the ashram. Dew-soaked sand was making *khus-khus* sound beneath my feet. Sometimes, my feet were getting locked in the wet sand. Lumps of wet sand also found their way inside my socks, making me feel even colder.

I was walking towards the west. On the other side, Allahabad fort was standing like a silhouette in the darkness. Through the gap in a tree, I could even see the flags fluttering on top of the fort. Perhaps, the moon had just set behind the fort. That is why there was a hint of light in the western sky.

The Kumbh-mela of lakhs of people was strangely silent now. The drone of the cricket, the murmuring sound of the ceaselessly flowing Ganga and the *khus-khus* sound of my footsteps—all mixed with the all-encompassing silence produced a music. As if, an invisible music aficionado was orchestrating this flow of music from somewhere.

Again, I heard that irregular sound of the bells very near. I stopped short and noticed that an elephant was tied a little farther from me. It was occasionally rocking its head the way a connoisseur moved his head in tune with music. The bells were as if keeping time with that tune.

A little farther away, smouldering smoke was rising from a few burnt logs. Obviously, a fire was made, but it had died away. Very near that 'fire place', a few persons were fast asleep, with their bodies covered from head to toe in blankets. I found it difficult to even imagine how anyone could sleep under the open sky in this dreadfully cold night.

Suddenly, an ear-splitting booming sound jolted me up. Looking north, I saw a train was climbing upon the railway bridge over the river Ganga. I imagined that this deep booming sound spreading in all directions would immediately wake up lakhs of people and the mela would come alive.

But as the sound of the train faded away, the sand-bed became totally calm again. And in this deep silence, I heard a broken voice telling somebody something.

I got curious. As I tried to listen more closely, I heard something, which sounded like a confession. Somebody was weeping and saying, 'I have committed a lot of sin. Oh God, take my wealth, my gold, my food. Disrobe me, take all that I have and give me death. I am laying down this sinful life at your feet. Accept it and liberate me.'

My hands and feet turned into lead. Whose confession was I hearing in this darkness? Whose desire for death? What is this place where people were unmasking their sin without hesitation and asking for death as punishment?

I forgot that I was a citizen of a civilized and cultured city. I felt as if I had been transported to a past era of thousand years ago. This dark night engaged me in an atavistic embrace on this vast stretch of sand and I started looking around frantically like a man possessed.

At a little distance, I could see the flame and fire on a fire-pit; perhaps the wood from the sacrificial fire of Sage Bharadwaj was still burning there. Hundreds of people have committed suicide by throwing themselves in the Ganga from time immemorial. Their wraiths, their shadows circled around me. Shadows from a forgotten age of Bharatvarsha. They were observing in amazement a little man clad in overcoat. Who was this creature, they perhaps thought. What was this man of flesh and blood doing in our nightly pasture of hundreds of years at the bank of the Ganga? They had noticed a lot of changes through history. The immortal banyan tree from whose branches a lot of people jumped down to sacrifice their lives were cut down at the order of Emperor Akbar. They had noticed that cruel deed standing at the confluence of Ganga and Yamuna. Even after that they had watched lakhs of men and women through hundreds of years knocked their heads on the remnants of that immortal banyan tree. They burst into laughter at this futile act. No one heard their laughter, of course. Their lips bent in derision when they noticed how these people threw coins in the water in their desire to appease the gods. How desperately these mortals wanted to continue to live! How carefully they tried to conceal their sins!

Today, they wondered who was this person trespassing into their nocturnal territory. Surrounding me, they were nudging at each other, whispering with one another. I tried to speak out, but my voice had choked. Sensing this, they laughed out in unison. The rhythm of their combined laughter sounded like music. The music of the warbling sound of water. Breaking out of the trance, I found that I was standing on the shore of the river. And someone was singing nearby. A woman's voice. My haunted mind got diverted in a different direction. The sweet tune of the song cast a different kind of spell on me. I realized that it was not a song, but a sloka being recited in tune:

Chirang nivasang na samikshate yo
Hyudarchittah pradadati cha kramat.
Kalpitarthangshcha dadati pungsah
Sa tirtharajo jayati Prayagah.

Following the voice, I took a few steps and came to an abrupt halt. A woman was standing, facing the river. It looked like she was wearing a sari. Her long loosened hair had cascaded down her back. A few rays of light from the distant pontoon bridge had fallen on her face, highlighting her straight nose, trembling lips and dark eye lashes.

A few moments later, a man covered from head to toe came and stood by her side. He also lent his voice to the recital of the hymn.

After some more time, another girl came, leading a little boy by his hand. There were luscious curves on her youthful body and a hint of smile on her lips. She and the boy also joined in reciting the hymn. Their chorus mingled with the murmuring sound of the Ganga.

After a little while, they all moved towards the confluence. Without any thought, I also followed them. As time passed, the northern wind turned crazy and hit me hard with the chill.

Suddenly, I felt someone was following me. As I looked back, a shadow quickly stepped behind a tent door. But I did not give it much thought.

It was difficult to guess the time of the night. The sky behind the fort was covered in deep darkness. Some hazy lines formed in the eastern sky like low hills. As if an invisible sculptor was curving a new scene with his chisel and hammer.

The team of four was walking slowly before me reciting the glory of Prayag. The tune was muted, but their Sanskrit pronunciation was perfect. Even this terrible cold could not distort their voice at all.

I was not sure why I was following them. I knew a little of the history of Prayag, but I did not much believe in the mythical stories of her glory. Unlike others, I had not spread a palmful of water from the Ganga on my head, immediately on reaching Prayag. And yet, I was walking behind the group of four. Their voice had attracted me. History had whispered in my ear.

The women of Bengali household worship *dhyala pyala* in the month of Shravan (July–August). They worship the earth and the vegetation. I can understand its import: O earth, be fertile, let every piece of your soil fill up with green grain. Be satisfied with my offering. I will serve you through my whole life. In this primitive culture, one can see humanity's struggle for survival. During the New Harvesting festival, *Nabanna*, I hear the glory of life, the song of the harvest.

But this sand-band is the playground of ancient history. The nostalgic land of the history of our religion. No one dives here into that ocean of memory. No one looks for knowledge. Why then this singing of the glory of a sand-bed, which is cut off from human habitat and its life? I have no perception of the spiritual in my mind. How would I understand it?

Yet I was walking like a man in trance. Gradually, the rows of tents were left behind. As if we had left a makeshift town behind. Now it was only an endless stretch of sand. My feet were stuck in deep sand, time and again. Sometimes, there were marshy grass patches on the sand. That grass was bending down under the power of the wind. The wind was getting stronger and stronger. It whistled in my ear. It hit me like whiplashes.

Now, the pace of the group of four became slower, but their chorus got louder. The sandy land was climbing down towards the river. The water was glistening in the subdued light. I stopped short, some thirty–forty feet behind them.

Then I noticed that the blanket-clad man walked away some distance, where the sand-band had taken a left bend. The elder woman also followed him. They could not be seen any longer. The boy and the younger girl remained there. Suddenly, in this bone-shattering cold, the boy got rid of his clothes and proceeded towards the water. Before I could register my pain at this religious torture of a child, another sight totally numbed my senses. The girl also took off her clothes. She was in no hurry. Even in this cold, she undressed slowly. Then she stood there for a few moments. Not very distinctly visible, but not quite hazy either. My civilized mind got a jolt. Should I look on? My eyelids shut automatically for a moment, then opened again. There was nothing around to hide myself. My mind rebelled. Why should I run away? I have not committed any sin.

But had she also not seen me? Under the open sky, with chilly wind all around, there she stood, her long and thick hair flowing in the wind, the bold curves of her body showing off clearly, her mild voice chanting the *stotras*. The whole world as if transformed in front of me.

She stepped down in the water. Her chanting became muted. Standing spellbound, I suddenly saw light all around.

Where was so much light coming from? In fact, I stood facing the west. Turning around, I saw the light of dawn appearing from behind the skyline of Pratisthanpur. The waves of water rushing towards me from the western side had their crest scintillating with light and shade. At this moment, the blue water of the Yamuna had turned jet black. At the far west, the shape of the railway bridge appeared against the sky. On the north, the foundation stones of the fort climbed as if from the river itself. The trees on the north bank of the Yamuna were swaying violently at the stormy wind, as if they wanted to jump into the river. Among all these, every flowing murmuring of the Yamuna sounded like the giggling of a naughty girl.

A little later, the tuneful chanting again re-emerged from the Ganga:

Devi Sureshwari Bhagawati Gange
Tribhuvantarini taral tarange.

From the invisible lap of the Ganga, first came out the boy. He was shivering violently, his teeth chattering loudly. In a quick movement, he covered himself with the dry clothes. She came out almost immediately after him. This time, she was more distinct. The vermillion colour of the dawn was reflecting on all the strong lines of her body. Her long wet hair cascaded down her shoulders. She was not shivering, but her voice chanting the hymn was slightly trembling.

I should avert my eyes. So I did. I did not have the devotion of a religious person. My eyes worship beauty in all forms.

Though I embarked on this journey to get swept away by the flood of religious sentiment, my urban self had not forsaken me. I had seen many nude paintings in my life: Venus of the foreign artists, naked pleasure women; also soulful nude-studies of many Indian artists. My eyes have also witnessed stark nakedness on the celluloid.

But this nudity! It was as unhesitant as this sky, this horizon, this Ganga and Yamuna. This nudity was situation-oblivious. It was so awe-inspiring and yet so wonderful.

I know I have strayed. But having lost my way, which age have I been transported to? Which bygone century of India? The Second World War brought for us the fumes of poison. I crossed the threshold of youth with that poison clouding my vision. Whichever way I turned my eyes, I saw a country full of wounds and injuries—poverty, starvation, exploitation and cries of agony! Yet I rushed into this journey to see more of life. But which age of my country's past brought this picture alive before my eyes? This is also the picture of my country. To see this is to see yourself.

Now all four of them had re-assembled and covered themselves with dry clothes. Having completed the invocation to Ganga, they were now reciting something else:

Pratah smarami bhavabhitimahartishantoi
Narayanan Garurhavahanamvajanabham.

They were walking towards me. I was slightly taken aback by seeing the lead man in the daylight. He had a huge pair of mustaches and a head full of unkempt hair. The eyes were also somewhat bloodshot. There was a rosary of rudraksh around his neck and two smaller rudraksh bands around his wrists. Both his ears were pierced and adorned with rudraksh rings. I got scared. Where would I flee if he chastised me for my voyeuristic conduct?

As they came nearer, the man observed me closely with suspicious eyes. But when they reached me, he stopped short. Breaking into an embarrassed smile, he asked me in a coarse voice, 'Are you not an army man?'

Me? Do I look like an army personnel? Oh, it may be the charisma of my overcoat.

I said, 'Not at all.'

He showed his large teeth in an expansive smile and said, 'Maharaj! I thought you are from the army. Namaskar, Maharaj, namaskar. Please give something to the sanyasi.'

My fear evaporated. This fellow wanted money. But I could not understand what kind of sanyasi he was, surrounded with women and child.

My disbelief perhaps sounded in my voice, 'What? You are a sanyasi?'

He roared in laughter. I felt as if the women and the child were silently praying.

Then he replied, 'Yes, Maharaj. I am an *avadhut*.'

Avadhut! I had heard the term, but did not know its meaning. They were a kind of mendicants. And who were these people with the sanyasi? I asked, 'Maharaj, what does *avadhut* exactly mean? Which kind of sect do you belong to?'

The sanyasi smiled and looked back. I also followed his glance. The young girl who held the hand of the boy was smiling bashfully with her head down. She looked a little embarrassed. She was hardly seventeen or eighteen, I guessed. The other woman was laughing openly. She looked straight at me without any embarrassment. It was difficult to gauge her age. She was rather plumb and well rounded. The boy was of about eight or nine years. To me, he was an oppressed being, with his shivering, his chanting and his sense of wonder.

If the rudraksha adornments were removed and normal clothes were given to wear, these women would immediately turn into ordinary housewives. If this laughter-radiant face was covered by the *pallu* of a sari, its appearance would change in a trice.

The sanyasi replied, 'Maharaj, I am short of time now. *Avadhut*s have a long history. I can tell you their story in a nutshell if you walk with us.'

I immediately agreed. Curiosity is a great motivator. I started walking with them towards the north again.

By that time, the fair was coming alive. Gradually, the din and bustle of activity was increasing. In some of the ashrams, morning prayer and reading of the Gita had started over the microphone.

The sanyasi said, 'In simple terms, a Shaivite monk is called an *avadhut*. There are further categories in it. Some *avadhuts* can be householders, some mendicants. I practice both methods. I can stay at home and I can renounce also. Then he suddenly asked me, 'How many forms of Lord Shiva can you see?'

I had no idea. So I simply replied, 'You tell me.'

The *avadhut* again broke out in a loud guffaw. Then he said, 'When he lives at home, he is a householder. When he goes out, he is a mendicant. Women are the ultimate goddesses, Maharaj. The *avadhuts* like me attain oneness with Lord Shiva if they succeed in their religious austerity.'

May be true. I have not had heard such strange things earlier. I asked the most obvious question, 'What's your relationship with these people?'

The sanyasi gestured at the grown-up woman and said, 'She is my partner. And the boy and the girl are my children. They haven't had their initiation yet.'

I got totally confused. I noticed that the young girl turned her face away with the hint of a smile. The boy had already forgotten his mantras and was looking at me with genuine curiosity. And the grown-up woman was looking at them with a light in the eye that comes from motherly affection only. Where was asceticism or renunciation in all this?

I asked, 'Do you manage through donation only?'

The sanyasi replied, 'There are not too many people these days who donate to a monk. I have my house. I also have some land. I earn my livelihood by farming. Now that I have come to a pilgrimage, begging alms is my only source of living.'

Though I was quite surprised by the mention of land and cultivation, I did not pursue the point. I asked instead, 'But I did not see any other monk or *avadhut*s taking a dip so early in the dawn.'

The sanyasi laughed, 'You've not seen, but many had taken a dip. Everything is not apparently visible. According to scriptures, this is Magha-*vrat*. A must for the *avadhuts*.

'I don't get you.'

'You didn't? From the day of Makar-sankranti, we are supposed to live on the sand-band of the Ganga. We have to keep fast and listen to the religious discourses. We have to talk about our own penances. Every dawn, we have to take a dip completely naked. Only then, the ultimate Brahman becomes satisfied.'

Taking a dip in cold water in this terrible winter just for satisfying Parama Brahman? Even if I give allowance for the initiated female *avadhut*, how do the teenaged girl and the boy go completely naked for taking a dip was beyond my comprehension. As I looked towards the girl again, she blushed. Like any bashful girl in any family, she covered her face and chest with the wave of her long disheveled hair.

We have reached the rows of tents. It was not possible for me to proceed any further. From the line of toilets, stench of phenyl and bleaching powder started invading my nostrils. I took out the wallet from my pocket. The eyes of the elder woman shone with a smile of gratitude. I gave some money to the *avadhut* and said, 'My resources are limited. This little donation…'

The sanyasi cut me immediately, bit his tongue and replied, 'No, Maharaj, never say anything like this. Whatever your kindness towards me is my Lord's kindness. Yours is the first face I have seen after my morning ablution today. Maybe one day, He had passed by me like this. Or He will. I would never want to know. Begging kindness is my begging alms.'

The smiling face of the avadhut turned serious. His eyes turned reddish and distant.

I just said, 'So long, then.'

He asked, 'Where do you stay here, Maharaj?'

I told him the name of my ashram. He asked again, 'Do you know the way to Tulsi-marg?'

I replied, 'No, I don't.'

He said, 'If you cross bridge no. 2, you will find Nirbani Ashram. The eastern road from there is called Tulsi-marg. After walking for a while, you would reach 108 Shankaracharya Ashram. Just behind that, I have my small hut. Visit us in the evening, please.'

I was a little bemused, as I could not gauge why he should be so eager to have me there. What kind of exchange was possible between him and a man like me who is non-religious and materialist by nature? I casually assured him that I would go if I found time.

Thanking me, he moved away with his group. The elderly woman also took leave of me with a smile, while the girl pulled at her brother's hand who was still gaping at me.

Even after bidding them goodbye, I kept standing there, thinking about the nature of the *avadhut*s. On the one hand, he was a total man, a father, a husband, a possessor of home and hearth. On the other, he was a God-intoxicated person, a seeker!

And his women? On the one hand, they were extremely shy and withdrawn. On the other hand, they could shed their clothes with complete indifference to the surroundings. Like the creepers growing upwards, they were one with Nature, as if their naked bodies were an offering to the sky.

But they are not creepers. They are women, our companions in life and death. We become curious at their strangeness, we give them company in their happiness, we empathize with their sorrow. But you cannot understand them by their external appearance. Nor you can possess them by touching with your hands. You need to touch them with your mind.

By now, the golden yellow sun had spread through the eastern horizon. Its warmth on this cold day felt rejuvenating. How sweet, how comforting! I knew when the season would change after a couple of months, I would curse this same sunlight as unbearable. This was the law of Nature.

As the sun rose, people started coming out of the tents. The long shadow of Jhusi fell upon the fairground. Sounds of human activities could now be heard all around. Rows of men and women were proceeding towards the river for the ritualistic dip. Noise of microphones chanting slokas and reading stotras was gathering tempo. At places, half-naked sadhus could be seen marching to the river in groups, shouting, 'Jai Mahadev ki jai', or 'Ram Ram Sita Ram', etc. From a long distance, the sound of drums and muted bugles came floating.

I have to make a move now. Rather than going back to the shelter of Didima and Pehlad, I better find a place for myself. With this thought, as I just turned around, I almost collided with Panch-Baidya. He was standing right behind me with his whole body covered in a thick blanket. I got a scare. He looked like an assassin who had been shadowing me all along. He was looking scary also, like the giant Frankenstein of the fiction. I wondered what harm I had caused him that he had been pursuing me like a tiger chasing a prey.

However, I tried to maintain a semblance of normalcy and asked with a smile, 'What news, Daktar-babu?'

The doctor was as if waiting for this question. Removing the blanket from his ferocious face, he challenged, 'I'm not just another doctor, but a *dhanvantari*. I know the remedy for all maladies.'

Well, why such an aggressive response to my humble question? There is a type of people in this world whom you cannot please either with good words or bad. In my boyhood, there was a boy called Becha who lived at the corner of our lane. I had never done any wrong to him. But whenever I would cross that corner, he would frown at me angrily, shout profanities and would even rain blows without any provocation. I was so terrorized that going out of home became a hazard. I could not confide in anyone because of my own vanity. I would only pray to Goddess Kali, 'O Mother, either shift the family of Becha to another locality or break both his hands.'

Panch-Baidya was like Becha. But in the kingdom of our boyhood, we ourselves were the nawabs, badshahs and caliphs. If you were weak, you had to owe allegiance to the stronger in whatever stranger terms of truce.

But was the story same here? I flew away from home like a pigeon, while the hunter falcon was sharpening its beak. Still I asked, 'Where are you going?'

The doctor raised his voice one rung and replied, 'Wherever I go, I am keeping an eye on you. Mind it.'

This time, I also reacted sharply, 'But why so?'

'That's my business.'

Having said so in a thundering tone, he thumped his chest heavily, raising a smoke of dust all around. I was angry, but I was embarrassed too. Everyone around was looking at us curiously.

I made a feeble attempt to stop him, but he continued in his booming voice, 'Do you think I didn't notice when you left the tent? Why did you leave the tent so late at night. Are there no rules and regulations?'

It was not possible on my part to match his voice. Still I asked defiantly, 'Why, is leaving the tent at late night forbidden by any rule?'

'Shut up. Just shut up. Didn't I warn you that I will teach you a lesson? I am Dr Panchugopal Roy.'

That's fine. But what was his reason for insulting me like this? Sheer madness? Gradually, a few curious onlookers were crowding in. After all, a fair has its standard characteristics. To stop this tirade, I said, 'Of course, you are not only a doctor, but a *dhanvantari*. Do whatever you want to do with me. But why are you screaming?'

'Of course, I will scream. It is my wish.'

The inevitable happened. A saffron-clad sadhu asked, '*Kya hua baba*? What has happened?'

It was like putting ghee in the fire. He threateningly advanced towards the sadhu, '*Jo hua so hua, tumko kya? Tum apna rasta dekho*. Whatever has happened, it's none of your business. Get lost.'

The polite smile of the mendicant evaporated in a moment. He fell silent with a sullen face.

The doctor raised his index finger in front of my face and said, 'How dare you pull my leg calling me *dhanvantari*?'

'Bah, it is you yourself—'

But who cared to listen? Where would I pour water if I did not know where the fire was?

The doctor was almost jumping in anger, 'Do you know that I am of your father's age?'

No surprise in this statement. I said, 'That's obvious. In which case, you should go home and chastise your own children. Why me?'

'Why, am I not supposed to have children?'

What incoherence of argument! Had I fallen in the grip of a total nut? Anyway, I responded, 'Why not? You can have a hundred children.'

'Hundred?

'Or may be two hundred?'

'Are you taunting me? Calling me a childless father?'

Even before I could rebuff him, the doctor collected his blanket around himself and started to walk off. His heavy steps were raising a cloud of dust as he stormed away like a mad buffalo. After going some distance, he turned back and shouted, 'So, you called me an impotent! Wait and see what I do to you.'

The doctor left. As if a storm had just subsided. I stood transfixed. I had no idea that after hitting the road, I would fall prey to such a crazy fellow. I thought I would drink life with both my eyes, would discover the rhythm of the world.

It dawned on me now that my expectations were lopsided. Why should Nature decorate the world for me with only azure sky, flowers in full bloom and birds chirping tunefully? Her multifaceted face is full of many contradictions. There are also the thunder and lightning, cloud and storm, mugginess and sweat. The other side of Nature.

I remembered how the doctor had silently entered the tent last night; his anguished comment at there being no place for him to sleep. And now, his last words, which were not only angry outburst, but also laced with an agony. In this apparent contradiction, there was some symmetry. I felt as if the doctor did not leave in a huff, but actually ran away. Ran away helplessly.

I looked at the receding figure of the man. I did not know why I felt that it was a great mistake to let him go. I should now try to catch him.

Meanwhile, a few men and women had assembled around me. They were trying to gauge my relationship with the doctor. Two persons speculated that these must be father and son; two others thought we could be two brothers. Go ahead, brother, patch up mutually between yourselves.

Right, now that I am on the stage, I have to take the cue; otherwise, why would the spectators leave me alone?

So, I would go and sort things out with the doctor. I started walking briskly.

The shops were opening. I had no time to watch the wares and goodies in different shops. Dodging through the crowd of men and women, I steadily gained upon the doctor. Once he was within the hearing distance, I shouted, 'Daktar-babu!'

He stopped short and looked back. He seemed to me like a palm tree, struck by lightning. He saw me and then again started walking with a faster pace.

I called out again, 'Please listen to me, Daktar-babu.'

But the doctor had climbed on to the bridge and was crossing to the other side. I persisted like a black guard. I had to catch him.

Finally, I caught up with him at the parade ground of the fort, on the other side of the Ganga. There was an assemblage of people for some reason. This had slowed down the doctor. On hearing me this time, he stopped and gave me a sidelong glance. It was the kind of glance a wild buffalo gives you before charging.

But what would I tell him? Though I ran after him for such a long time, now I felt tongue-tied.

As I was trying to think up something, my attention was drawn to the crowd. It had gathered around a huge motor car.

A song was blasting from a record player from inside the car: a drunken female singer was telling you, '*Hum peeke aye,*' followed by a hiccup. A hand was distributing something from inside the car. Lo and behold, it was steaming hot cups of tea and it was written in colour on the car, 'Annapurna Women's Restaurant.' Where had it come from? Delhi or Lucknow? A mobile cafeteria on the bank of the Yamuna? Some well-dressed men and women were seated on folding chairs and tables and enjoying hot tea on a cold morning. On the other side, a cashier sat on a table-chair with a coupon book. A hefty, bald gentleman—his fingers were shivering in the cold.

On a brainwave, I blurted out, 'Would you like a cup of tea, Daktar-babu?'

The doctor was speechless. As he was looking at me sidelong, he looked at the Annapurna car similarly, also at the majlis of tea. Then his eyes got fixed on the food items displayed on the showcase.

Silence is acquiescence. I said, 'Just wait. Let me buy the coupons.'

When I returned with two dishes of snacks, the doctor was not to be seen. I was a little disappointed. Was he not gazing at the food items wishfully? How could he leave then? As I turned towards the majlis, I found him occupying a chair and openly ogling at the young girl sitting on another chair, drinking tea. Squirming under the aggressive stare of the doctor, she was almost gulping down her tea. I put the food dishes down on the table and went away again to bring water and tea. There was a longish queue in front of the tea counter. As I stood in the queue, I was surprised to discover that I was not at all irritated. On the contrary, I was enjoying the moment, as if the mood of the fair was catching up. As I looked around, I found that cheery mood reflected everywhere.

Annapurna car's crazy music of '*Hum pee ke aye*' had ended. Suddenly, an age-old Bengali song started playing, but the accompanying static noises almost drowned the original song. I could still make out the lyric, *Praner prabhu rahe prane roy na bahirey* (The lord of my life remains within, not without).'

But who cared for the lyric and its meaning? What was needed was a sound in the background. On the other side, the sound of cymbals and drumbeats were getting louder and louder. From atop the embankment, thousands of people were coming down, like endless rows of ants. They were coming with bag and baggage. They were coming in tongas and rickshaws, on horses and donkeys, in lorries and private cars. From horizon to horizon, it was only men and women, of various colours, wearing various clothes, speaking various languages, singing various songs.

Even in the midst of that din and bustle, a few high-pitched voices were heard surprisingly clearly: '*Hey babu-bhaiya panch lok, hey dharma-baba*', the prayer of the beggar or '*Amrut, ley sasta amrut*', the hawking of the ferrywala selling cheap guava. *Amrut* and puri. Puri and *peda*. *Peda* and *moomphali*. I could see that the police were occasionally chasing the hawkers. Shopowners had paid thousands of rupees to obtain license for setting shop. Hawkers' entry was, therefore, illegal trespassing. But how far could you drive them out? There were no walls, no gates. The Sangam land was an open area. So, when chased, they easily moved from one side to the other. Wherever you went, there were people. And people meant potential buyers. The visitors to the fair had money in their pocket. And they had hunger in their belly. That was enough.

The queue for tea, in which I was standing, exhibited another face of the Kumbh-mela. The men and women here were wearing dazzling woollen garments. The menfolk sported expensive Western suits. Even in this early morning, roses and lipsticks were eminently on display. Albert fashion hairstyle was the go of the day. Obviously, the fashion statement here was inspired by Hollywood/Bollywood. Gregory Peck and Susan Haward. Dilip Kumar and Madhubala.

Of course, like me, there were other exceptions in the queue. *Nagra chappal*-wearing Rajasthanis, Sikhs with dense facial beard, women with twelve-yard sarees and matching cholis. They could not laugh enough. Tickets for tea? Strange world! Is this the way gentlemen-shopkeepers sell tea? *Arré Ram kaho, Ram kaho.*

In front of me, there was a suited-booted young man and a fashionably dressed young woman. Must be husband and wife. It seemed they were interested in music. The woman attentively listened to the metallic noise and said, 'Perhaps an

Odia song.' The young man responded, 'It sounds Madrasi to me.' I was dumb-struck by their linguistic expertise. However indistinct it might be, did '*Praner prabhu rahe prane*' sound like Odia or Madrasi? I could only lament at the fate of my mother tongue.

I rushed back to our table with two cups of tea. Good God, the doctor was still glaring at the other occupant of the table—the pretty-looking young woman. The touch of the surma, the collyrium in her eyes was quite distinct. She was smarting under the gaze of the doctor, just as the hunted smarts at the gaze of the hunter. As I reached the table, she looked up at me with relief. Her eyes as if tried to tell me, 'What sort of man are you? Have left behind a nut alone here.' Even unknown people often speak through their eyes.

The woman hastily left the table without finishing her tea. The doctor seemed to be more at ease now. He kept the folded blanket on a chair and took a sip of tea from the cup. A little later he attacked the food from the plate. The more he ate, the more the hard lines from his face retreated. It turned unbelievably soft. As if a humane expression on the face of Frankenstein lit up the doctor's face, as if a magic wand had touched it.

Housewives often say, 'It's a pleasure to watch someone eating at their heart's content.' Perhaps this is what they meant. I had never felt so much happiness by feeding somebody. I forgot to touch my plate.

The doctor finished both the plates. Then he seemed to be feeling a little embarrassed. He was averting from my gaze. I closely watched his face. His thick lips were now moist. The skin of his otherwise rough and rugged face was looking smooth. His head was full of unkempt salt-and-pepper hair. His dress was darned and mended at many places. He had a decidedly strong physique, but how pitiable the face was.

I went to the cashier again and bought two more plates of food. Though I was on a shoestring budget, I thought it was a rare opportunity to satisfy the soul. Maybe, I got a little carried away by emotion.

On seeing more food, the doctor looked at me searchingly. Perhaps, he tried to gauge if I had got angry again.

I said, 'Eat.'

He looked at the food and at me. The he dragged one plate towards himself. After he finished this, I said, 'The other plate is also for you.'

At last, he broke his vow of silence and asked, 'What about you?'

'I will take only tea.'

But the doctor did not touch the other plate. He took out a small chillum from inside his trouser pocket. It was a bright red chillum for smoking ganja. From other pockets, he fished out a downy fibre of jute and coconut coir. When he realized that these would not work, he kept them back in the pockets and asked, 'Do you have a bidi or something?'

I took out a cigarette from my pocket. Obviously, he was not particularly fond of it.

I asked, 'Are you satiated?'

He said, 'Never. Has anybody ever been satiated? And how would that happen to me?'

At my surprised look, the doctor said, 'What little food Pellad's grandma used to give me till yesterday, you jeopardized that also.'

'Me? How come?'

The doctor almost reverted to his grumpy self again, and said, 'You endeared yourself with her at the cost of my position. She is stingy. In fact, all these old women are stingy. I have brought sixteen such oldies from Bengal to Kumbh, virtually on my shoulder. What sweet talk then! All are paving the road to heaven on Panchugopal's shoulders! I will also give them back. No one is physically going to heaven. A time will come when they have to return to their homes. Will see how they do it.'

I asked, 'You've brought them?'

'Who else? Who knows all the tricks other than Panchugopal? It is I who have fixed their tents through my own connection.'

The doctor worked himself up to a foul mood again and thundered as if I was the culprit, 'And this was not just a verbal arrangement. There is a proper signed contract. They are supposed to provide me food twice and a sleeping berth in one of the tents by turn. Now, what to speak of food, they did not even provide me a little space within the tent to sleep!'

I was pained to hear this story. I could not have even imagined that the doctor did not have provision for two meals a day and a shelter at the night. Now I remembered his stealthy entry into the camp last night and the disgustful muttering, 'No room, nothing!' But the mystery of Panchugopal intrigued me. How did a doctor turn into a small time travel agent?

I felt guilty for the last night. True that I was the trespasser who perhaps pushed him away unwittingly. It is I who had kept him hungry and shelterless. I tried to apologize by saying, 'I am really sorry for the last night…'

'You?' The doctor almost pulled me up, 'What have you got to do with it? I've long ceased to react to such trivia. Come on, did you think I was sulking against you? Ha! My heart is much larger. It is not for nothing that I was a mendicant for ten years and travelled throughout the country.'

'You became a sadhu?' I asked, incredulously.

'Yes, very much.'

'Why?'

'Well, no particular reason. He dragged me out of my home. Perforce.'

'Who?'

'Who else? The quest inside. The search.'

'Then why did you abandon that life?'

'I haven't abandoned anything, just as I had not embraced anything. I put on a loin-cloth. Just threw it away. The lust for life forces you out. It is the same lust for life that brings you back.'

Having declared that, the doctor looked straight into my eyes for the first time. I saw deep distress and agony in them. He asked me, 'Tell me, does the quest ever leave you?'

I did not know the answer. But I was not aware that inadvertently, I had turned the key on a rusty lock after a long time. The doctor started talking torrentially, 'Where have I not gone? Braving the snow of the thick winter I have climbed the Himalayas. Even the wild animals ran away, but I did not give up. Cowardly priests and sadhus did not open the temple doors, lest they had to feed me. But I ignored all the mundane necessities of life and death; physical hunger and thirst did not matter to me. Yet, was the other thirst ever quenched? No.'

I called out, 'Daktar-babu?'

He was immediately incensed, 'Daktar-babu? Are you making fun of me? I have never studied medicine. I am a quack who sells herbs and drugs. I hawk these on the street. I prepare and sell ointment for scabies and ringworms. Amulet? Yes, I prescribe that too. But how dare you call me a doctor?'

I was in a fix. There was no point reminding him that he himself had used the prefix 'doctor' yesterday. Reminding it might further aggravate his mood. As such, some tea enthusiasts were already looking at us because of his loud voice. I guessed correctly that Panchugopal's embarrassment lay in others' addressing him as doctor. It was a cruel joke.

This time, I called, 'Panchugopal-babu!'

The doctor looked at me. I was quite flummoxed to see that he was actually smiling. In his terrible face, huge teeth were looking almost threatening.

He said, 'So, you are making sweet talk. Back brushed hair, calm pair of eyes, goody-goody face. I know your type quite well.'

I did not object. By now I had learned that contradicting him might produce an unpredictable effect. In a low tone, the doctor said, 'Look at her, just leaving the other table. Large eyes, sharp nose, lovely face. Apparently a very homely girl.'

I understood whom he was referring to. I ventured, 'Yes, I have noticed her. Quite a dignified lady.'

The doctor cut me short, 'Don't you dare give a certificate. Such types are dangerous. They can do anything.'

I was taken aback by this harsh judgment without any apparent basis.

The doctor said, 'So, you are not convinced, right?'

He fished out a dirty paper from his pocket. It was creased from much folding. Very carefully, the doctor unravelled a bright photograph from inside the paper. He put the photograph in front of me and asked, 'How is she?'

'Beautiful!'

I was not making up. It was a lovely face—dark eyes with long lashes, sharp nose, locks of hair dangling on the smooth forehead. It was difficult to guess the exact age, but she was young, very young.

Now came the invective. The doctor said in distaste, 'Poison, terrible poison, beautiful poison.'

With a lot of trepidation, I asked, 'Who is she?'

The doctor did not reply immediately. He was looking at the terrible, beautiful poison of his affection. His face softened down like it did when he looked at the plates of food. His deep-set eyes brightened up as he looked at the photograph.

At the next moment, he folded the photograph in the paper and said, 'You were asking about her identity. My wife died giving birth to her.'

'Your daughter?'

I guessed he was unwilling to use the term 'my daughter'.

There was laughter and merry-making all around. The chorus of horse's neighing and coughing of motor cars. In this din, Panchugopal's usual grating voice sounded very soft, as if somebody was playing on the lower notes of a clarinet.

He said, 'You won't believe that the mother of that girl in photograph was even more beautiful. Look at the face in front of you, that of Panchugopal Roy, son of Prangopal Roy. How ugly I am! Looking at my appearance, people shun my company. And yet, she was in deep love with me. She loved me so much that occasionally, even I would get confused. She would fuss over my food, over my rest and all that. But she passed away giving birth to that girl. Before I could even value the worth of her love, she left. Like a mad man, I thought somebody has made a conspiracy to hide her from me. I looked for her all around, forlorn and disoriented. But how long does a man's grief-stricken madness last? One day, looking at the mattress in my home, I suddenly felt she herself was manifest in the smiling face of my daughter. Till then, I had neglected her. The women of the locality had been bringing her up. Now I took charge. Gradually, she started crawling, laughing, walking, blabbering. I named her Sheuli, as she was as beautiful as the *sheuli* (night-flowering jasmine) flower. Soft and sweet. I used to work in a factory, but would eagerly wait for the duty hours to be over so that I would rush to hold her in my embrace. She was the cynosure of my eyes, my love and affection, my heaven and goddess. She was at the centre of my existence. I would clad her like a princess, much to the amusement of my friends and neighbours. As she grew up, I put her in a school with much reluctance. She had a very sweet voice and I dreamt of grooming her up as a singer. She was like a flower blossoming in my private garden.'

At this point, Panchugopal paused for a moment. I wondered at his unsuspected ability to speak in such poetic manner. Anyway, he lowered his tone one notch and continued, 'She turned seventeen. A full-blown young girl. But she was calm and collected. No fickleness anywhere. Like her mother. I was not just her father, but her friend too. Whenever there was any talk of marriage, she would place her head on my chest and declare, 'Papa, I can never stay away from you.'

After saying this, Panchugopal suddenly stopped, as if a car had abruptly braked. Looking at him, I saw that his face had distorted in pain and rage. He spat out the last words, 'All a lie. She was a devil. There was poison in her beauty. One day, she left. Without even giving any hint to me, she eloped with a boy. A boy from our mohalla.'

The ending of the story coincided dramatically with the curtain coming down on Annapurna's makeshift tea stall.

The bearers came to fold up the tables and chairs. I did not notice when the music had stopped.

We got up and started walking towards the bridge. Panchugopal was silent. There was no need to talk either. All his apparent contradiction in behaviour, his bitter aversion towards young and beautiful girls, his sudden mood swings, his vagabond life as a mendicant and his search now made some sense to me. He himself had talked about the burning inside him. Neither the oceans, nor the Himalayas could douse the fire that burnt inside his heart.

After crossing the bridge, we stood by the side of the Ganga. Serpentine footprints could be seen on the sandbank. Gurgling sound of the water could be heard.

I asked softly, 'Panchugopal-babu, where is your daughter now?'

He replied with a sigh, 'Wish I knew it. Couldn't she have sent me a message from wherever she is? I have been searching for the last ten years, but could not find a trace.'

There was a long silence. I had to make a move. Had to search for a shelter. Our searches never end. Panchugopal's might continue for the rest of his life. As I was about to take leave, he suddenly turned his face and asked, 'What do you do for a livelihood?'

It was always a tough question for me. I was never sure if the work I did was at all presentable. People immediately started judging. Still I decided to tell Panchugopal the truth.

'I am a writer.'

Panchugopal was surprised, 'What do you write? Books?'

I shrank at his astonishment. Was writing books a sin? I managed to say. 'Yes.'

'What kind of books? Of knowledge? Or stories and novels?'

I could sense that he would be happier if I had written books of knowledge. But I had to be truthful, 'Novels and short stories, usually.'

Panchugopal said, 'I guessed as much. I am sure there is an earning father to support you.'

'Why do you say so?'

'Otherwise, how do you make both ends meet?'

I was stumped. Yet I protested, 'Why, are not the writers in Bengal surviving?'

Panchugopal said, 'Our Keshtokanta lives on his father, along with his wife and children, and write books after books.'

I asked, 'Who is Keshtokanta?'

'A young man of our locality.'

I said, 'May be. But my father has passed away long back.'

Panchugopal was more surprised. He said, 'You do not even part your hair fashonably.'

'Why should I?'

Keshtokanta says, 'If you want to be a writer, you have to part your hair in style, have to wear a pair of gold-rimmed spectacles and always sport a stole on your shoulder.'

I scanned Panchugopal's face. He was not pulling my leg. He made this statement with innocent faith.

I did not know who Keshtokanta was, nor did I have the great fortune of reading his books. So, I said, 'Everyone doesn't follow one model. Perhaps, your Keshtokanta likes such trappings.'

Panchugopal said, 'Huuuum', which may mean many things. Then he asked again, 'And how long have you been in this business?'

'What business?'

'This moving around in pilgrimages?'

I said, 'This is the first time.'

Panchugopal nodded his head knowingly, 'That's why you went out alone so late at night.'

'Why, is it not advisable?'

'Some night they will break your neck and bury you under the ground.'

Bury me? Why? What is my crime?

I asked, 'Who will want to do that? And why?'

Panchugopal laughed for the second time in the day. Then he said, 'One who needs to do it. I guess you have money in your pocket.'

Money? Yes, I have some. Now I began to understand what he was driving at.

Panchugopal suddenly turned serious, 'Look, dangerous people are lurking around at every corner in these few miles. Many of them are in the garb of sadhus. They would not miss an opportunity to rob you. And never interact with sadhus at night.'

I remonstrated, 'But last night I did not notice anything like that.'

'It does not happen all the time. Moreover, last night I was behind you like a shadow. Let me warn you about something else. There are many sirens here. They would also not lose a chance to lure you.'

Now Panchugopal almost started scaring me. I said, 'Sirens? Who are they?

Panchugopal said with distaste, 'If you find any such creature, your eyes will get locked with hers. She will cast side-long glances, will smile mischievously. You will feel as if she is beckoning you to her breast. Be wary of such creatures, understand?'

Turning his face, he muttered to himself, 'I've seen it all. In the last Kumbh at Hardwar, three young men were murdered. All from educated middle class families like you.'

I was a little scared. Obviously, Panchugopal was much more experienced than me in this field. I could not rubbish his words.

Still I said, 'All this in such a pilgrim's place?'

He said, 'It is easier here. Since it is a pilgrim's place, you cannot stop anyone from coming here. You will see a lot. I will show you. Do you drink?'

Alcohol? I said, 'No. Why?'

'You will get everything here. Illegal brews are aplenty around.'

Gradually, I started getting the picture. Even in this pilgrim's place, there were makeshift brothels, there are secret country-liquor shops. At least, that was what Panchugopal was hinting at. I could not altogether pooh-pooh him away. Human beings are capable of everything.

Before taking leave of him, I asked, 'Can you tell me where are other Bengali ashrams here?

Panchugopal said, 'They are everywhere. Why?'

'I will have to find out an alternative shelter.'

'Why, don't you want to continue to stay in that camp?'

I said, 'How could I? I sought shelter only for the last night. Today I should look for a new place to stay.'

Panchugopal stared at me with hurt eyes and said, 'I see. You've been plotting all this throughout. That's why you've been talking to me so graciously so long.'

I was stunned by Panchugopal's sentimental reaction. It is the same man who last night tried his best to drive me out of that tent. There was no point reminding him of this fact. He was driven by the heart-felt emotion of the moment. He now asked me in a cold voice, 'Who had made you take an oath that you must leave that camp after one night?'

I said, 'No one has. But I have a sense of propriety.'

Panchugopal worked up a temper, 'To hell with your propriety! Once the old hag has given you shelter, she will not ask you to leave. Just go and pay the old woman some cash for your food and stay. You won't have any further problem.'

Then again, he muttered within himself, 'First time in this business. That's why you are unduly bothered with non-issues.'

I was still in two minds. I thought of spending a few days without any inhibition. I would move around freely. Would not staying in Pehlad's camp rob me of my freedom? Of my peace of mind?

Suddenly, Panchugopal turned towards me and said fiercely, 'Listen, I don't believe that goody-goody boys like you turn out to be real good fellows. But I will be extremely distressed if you leave that tent. Understand?'

Saying so, he completely turned around, obviously to hide his emotions from me.

The situation was almost ludicrous. But I could not laugh. This was humanity. It is in search of such minds that I had left home and hit the road. Who knew that I would meet such a gentle giant like Panchugopal in the courtyard of Kumbh-mela?

Finally, I said, 'Ok, then let's go.'

He looked at me surreptitiously and started walking slowly. I took out my cigarette packet and offered him one. He declined, saying, 'This does not work for me. If you like, you can give me two annas. I will indulge in some real intoxication.'

I gave him the two annas, but was not sure where he would find hemp here. Panchugopal looked around and called out to a sadhu, saying, 'Hey, Baba.' The sadhu paused, even in the push and pull of the crowd and asked, 'What, my son?'

Panchugopal said, 'I need your little blessing, Baba.'

The sadhu came nearer. Panchugopal handed over the two annas and said, 'Bless me with a bit of *saptami*, Baba. It is difficult to go to the town now.'

The sadhu looked at me suspiciously and asked, 'Which *jamat*?'

Panchugopal replied, 'Now I am a householder, Baba. In search of a new guru. Have left my earlier guru.'

The sadhu made a sympathetic sound with his tongue and said, 'Go and meet Vishnu Brahmachari in his ashram. You will find your guru.'

Then he fished out a small packet from his *jhola* and passed it on to Panchugopal.

As the sadhu left, I asked him, 'What is *saptami*?'

Panchugopal said, 'The smoke of Mahadev. The hemp. Among many sects, hemp is called by that name.'

Then he made a derisive gesture and said, 'Ha! He wants me to search for a guru at Vishnu Brahmachari's ashram. No way. I've seen it all.'

I did not quite comprehend the matter, but could not ask Panchugopal its meaning, as he got busy preparing the hemp for smoking.

After a fifteen minutes walk, we reached the camp. It was full of activities.

On one side, cooking was going on. On another, religious precepts over the microphone. The scene was full of verve.

Prahlad came rushing forward and said, 'Well, you people are having a great time. And here I am withering away in absence of a puff.'

Even before I could protest, Panchugopal shouted at him, saying, 'Don't shoot your mouth without knowing anything. This boy is not in our racket. He paid me two annas, with which I have managed my puff.'

Prahlad was overjoyed at this turn of events. He said, 'Oh really! He is not a *rasika*, right? But doctor-uncle, I am dying for a puff.'

Panchugopal extended his palm and demanded, 'First things first. Drop a few annas and have your fill.'

Prahlad immediately obliged. Keeping the coins in his pocket, Panchugopal commanded, 'Now follow me.' And they vanished in search of their high.

I was wondering how little we knew of other people's minds. Thinking of Panchugopal brought a bemused smile on my lips. Someone said, 'What are you smiling at?'

I looked and found that the saffron-clad sanyasi of the last night was standing before me.

I said, 'Smiling at Panchugopal's strange ways.'

'You already thick with him?'

'Well, to some extent.'

'He was in our ashram at Kashi for three years at a stretch. The fellow is completely mad. He became a sadhu at that time and troubled all of us to no end.'

The sanyasi continued, 'Of course, last night I came to stop you from entering the tent because of his complaint. These are our duties, you know.'

'Yes, of course.'

'Moreover, I am responsible for your comfort in the ashram. You can say that I am both the accountant and the manager in this ashram.'

I got curious on hearing this. I asked him, 'So, you also have a kind of bureaucracy?'

'Of course we have. One has to have all this paraphernalia for running an establishment. Officer, manager, clerk—everything. Especially when we congregate outside, we have to follow the hierarchy. First the Mohanta, then the priest, followed by accountant, administrator, stock-in-charge, guards, band-player—the whole works. Do you think the discipline in these ashrams happens automatically? No way, people have to work hard to achieve this.'

I was suitably impressed. Didn't know that such huge administrative machinery worked in a religious ashram also. It sounded like the ways of the work-a-day world, like that of the society, even like that of the state.

I said, 'How come you also have all these rules and regulations? These are meant for us, common people.'

'Why should not there be rules and regulations? The whole world has its set of rules. The sun rises and sets. Day follows night. Season changes. If you need to earn, don't you run to the office in the morning as a matter of rule? Don't you open your shop at a given time every day? Only in case of realizing your God, you don't expect any rule. Why, is not the other world also governed by a set of rules?'

'But we had always been told that the *siddha*s who had realized Godheads in their hearts were beyond time and space. They live by their own whims. It was beyond common people's comprehension what they would do and where and when?'

The sanyasi laughed and said, '*Siddha*s? They are few and far between. How many of all the sadhus, sanyasins and yogis have attained Godhead from among the vast multitude that have assembled here in the Kumbh-mela? And who would recognize that such a person has attained salvation? Who would know where he is roaming around and under which guise?'

Suddenly, the smiling face of the sanyasi turned grave. He folded his palms and said, 'Wherever he is, he has to come here. He has no way to avoid the Kumbh of Prayag at the month of Magh. But how does one recognize him? Maybe, the Mohanta with whom I have been moving around for years is that man.'

Having said so, he looked at me intently and declared, with a curious smile, 'Maybe, he is walking around wearing a trouser and an overcoat like you. How do I know?'

Early this morning, I have heard a similar sentiment in the voice of the *avadhut* also. Nobody knew when would God pass you, in which guise. It seemed that such a belief was there in everybody's mind. There was a strange emotion and devotion in such a belief. While uttering this belief, a person usually got a little transformed. Hence, any comment from my side would be totally uncalled for. I remained silent.

The sanyasi himself reverted to his normal suave self and told me in a clear voice, 'Leave all this discussion for another occasion. Ramjidasi is coming to our ashram this afternoon. Please do not go away from the ashram.'

I asked, 'Who is she?'

'Haven't you heard of her? She is a *sadhika*. She takes turn to visit one ashram every day. She has sent word that today she would come to us. We have been announcing it in the loudspeaker at regular intervals. She hails from Himachal Pradesh. You will feel her charisma once you see her. Anyway, I would not detain you any more.'

He made for the door, then turned again and asked, 'Hope you will recognize your tent, won't you?'

Why should not I? Then I looked towards the rows of tents. Good heavens! All looked alike and stood in rows without any gap. I got out at the small hours of the morning. Didn't notice any landmark. They were looking like housing blocks of the railway colonies. You peep in the wrong house and hear abuses.

The saffron-clad kotwal smiled at my confusion and said, 'At the beginning, such confusion is natural. Do you see that old woman sitting in front of a tent. The one on the right of it is yours. You will see "No. 12" written in Hindi on it with chalk.'

I thanked him and said, 'Without you I surely would have faced trouble. But may I ask you something else?'

He said, 'Go ahead.'

I asked, 'Are you a Bengali?'

The kotwal laughed meaningfully and said, 'Does it really matter? Yes, I am a Bengali. Was born somewhere in Bengal. Look, human curiosity is endless. I may not be able to reply to all your questions.'

He went away flashing a smile, virtually cautioning me not to ask too many questions. A strange person indeed!

On the raised platform, the Mohanta was seated on the stage. By his side, a singer was tuning his voice with the tanpura. Usually, after a song was rendered, the Mohanta would talk about religion, about the pious way of life, for some time. There was a sizeable gathering listening to him. Apart from the boarders of this ashram, there were people from outside also. One was supposed to listen to religious talks and devotional songs in a pilgrimage. Small talks and gossips were also going on. Five or six Punjabi women were talking and laughing on one side. With their colourful kurta-pyjamas and dupattas, they were looking like a fully blossomed bunch of flowers. There were the jingling sound of a hundred ankle-bells in their spontaneous laughter. That unruffled a few senior ladies, who were piercing them with disapproving looks. Their unuttered message was, 'If you wish to laugh, why don't you go outside?'

The ashram is spread over a few bighas of land. A number of carefree children were playing on the open area. Their mirthful laughter and shouting was adding another dimension to the ashram's otherwise solemn atmosphere. On the other hand, the agreeing aroma of ghee was flowing in the wind. Along with it, was there a whiff of familiar spices typically used in Bengali dishes?

Reaching in front of the tent, I had another problem. Half of the tent belonged to another group. Now, which one was ours? Perhaps the one on the left. I tentatively raised the canvas cover and found a very young girl knelt down on the floor. She was wearing a coloured handloom sari over her frock. Her braided hair was hanging on her shoulder. It seemed she was chewing something with great relish and muttering a tune under her breath. Was there a smearing of vermillion at the parting of her hair? Is she a Bengali, then?

Suddenly, the girl saw me. Her reaction was ludicrous. She uttered a suppressed cry and sprang up on her feet. Simultaneously, she released the corner of the sari and covered her head. A bunch of ripe brown jujube fell down from her lap and spread on the floor.

Good heavens, it was the wife of our Prahlad! I felt no remorse for disturbing her privacy. I was rather amused and at the same time, amazed. How can such a chit of a girl feel and express so much abashment at being spied by a stranger! At her age, the children of our country usually sat with their teacher-madams with a pencil and a slate. Of course, their playthings were gender-oriented. They even played the role of a future mother-in-law while organizing the marriage of their dolls. They even play bride-bride in mock marriages.

But this girl was a real-life child bride. I had seen her yesterday also, but as her face was always covered, I could never imagine that she was so young. Finally, I broke the spell and said awkwardly, 'Why don't you collect the jujubes from the floor?'

She immediately obeyed me and picked up the fruits on the loose end of her sari. As I took off my overcoat, I said, 'You can eat them while I change.'

She did not reply, but from inside her make-shift veil she was looking at me with intent eyes. I was wondering if I should start a conversation with her and find out about the arrangement of bath and food. But before I could make up my mind, something strange happened. The girl moved away and stood near the outer screen and shot at me angrily, 'Where did you vanish so early in the morning? Let Di'ma come, you'll feel the heat.'

Blurting this out, she vanished in a trice. I froze at the half-executed action of taking off my shirt. This was perhaps what is called pulling up someone. Or was it a declaration of war? While I was apprehensive that this shy girl with her face fully covered might break down in tears at the possible loss of her berries, she turned out to be quite a bundle of energy. There was real steel in her voice. Outside, the preceptor was explaining the text of the Mandukyopanishad and inside, I crazily burst out in a loud laughter at my own predicament.

A little later, she came back. Her face was as covered as before. She kept a small bottle of mustard oil in front of me and then sat down in one corner. Again, that tone of chastisement was heard, 'Go and take your bath quickly. Di'ma has instructed. Or else...'

But how could I rub oil on my body? Were not oil and soap banned in a pilgrim's place?

I asked, 'Who sent the oil? Didima?'

She was silent for a moment, then replied in a hushed tone, 'No, I have brought it. Use it quickly. If Di'ma finds out, she will curse me.'

So, she was secretly favouring me! This wife of Prahlad seemed to have a lot of compassion and good sense. I could no longer ignore her as a shy, backward village wench.

As desired by her, I quickly sat down and started rubbing oil on my bare torso. While doing so, I asked, 'What's Didima doing?'

The girl seemed to have a mercurial temper. She replied sharply, 'What else? Cooking, cleaning, working. She is not like you who keeps roving about like a vagabond the whole day.'

As her retort ended, I heard a cracking sound from inside her head cover. I could guess that she had taken a healthy bite into a ripe jujube.

But why so much rebuke? Was it meant for the absentee Prahlad? Perhaps for both of us. But I had started enjoying it. I left home in search of variety, in search of stranger things. And here I was, discovering this strange variety at a Bengali child-bride from near home. Perhaps, we did not know how to look around us.

With not a little apprehension, I asked, 'May I know your name?'

I saw a flash of her disapproving eyes which, as if, was trying to say, 'It's not proper to ask the name of a married woman.'

But loudly she said, 'Shrimati Brajabala Devi.'

It was not possible for me to call her using such a tough name.

So, I said, 'Okay, I'll then call you Bouthan, as others do.'

'Bouthan?' She uttered the word in a conspiratorial whisper and broke out in a giggle. The word had made her mighty happy. Meanwhile, her head cover had slipped off.

Her demeanour became serious again. Slightly bending down, she said in a muffled tone, her eyes animated with expression, 'There is a very stingy old woman here, you know. She will surely ask money from you. That she does with everyone. But people say that the old hag already has a lot of money. Don't give her any money, I tell you.'

I said, 'Is that so?' Then declared gravely, 'Would never give her even a paise.'

Now, the head covering had come down on the shoulder. But Brajabala was oblivious to it. Perhaps, she had found a companion after a long time. She needed to talk. In the same hushed tone, she again said, 'You know, a very beautiful woman had come here. What a face, what eyes! Her cascading hair is even longer than mine. But she doesn't talk to anyone. Do you know why?'

Taken aback by the sudden question, I mumbled, 'No, I've no idea. Sorry.'

Seeing me embarrassed, Brajabala made a sympathic pout of her lips and said, 'You know nothing. They say, the woman's husband had become a sadhu ten years back and left home. So, she had come with her brother-in-law to look for him. You know this is the place where all sadhus converge.'

I had not seen that mute beauty, nor did I know anything about her. So, I could only express my sense of wonder, saying, 'Is that so?'

There was a pained expression in Braja's tender face. She said, 'Yes, I myself have seen her. I'll try to secretly show her to you.'

Watching a woman secretly may not be a very civilized move. Still I had to acquiesce, saying, 'Okay.'

But Brajabala was not done yet. Her eyes and face sparkled like a rainbow everytime she moved to a different line of conversation. Suddenly, she visibly shrank with fear and said, 'You know, there are a lot of thieves around here.'

Before I could gauge if thieves had stolen any of her belongings, her mood changed and she broke into an uncontrollable laughter, perhaps remembering something. Looking at my askance face, she said, 'This morning everyone ran after a thief. A female thief.'

So, Brajabala was a gazetteer also. I asked, 'How do you know that the thief was a woman?'

Now, she released the seed of jujube from her mouth and replied with wonder in her eyes, 'Everyone said so. Besides, she came again. Haven't you seen that the thief has made a big hole on the eastern fence. She poked her head through the hole. Someone saw her face by chance. So, she again fled.' At this stage, Brajabala lowered her voice almost conspiratorially and said, 'People say that the thief is a fallen woman. If they can catch her, they will hand her over to the police.'

I do not know if one could be doubly serious. I feigned astonishment and said for the umpteenth time, 'Is that so?'

Braja turned her slender neck in a delectable pose and declared, 'Yes, dear.'

The very next moment, Brajabala's eyes blazed with fire and she said, 'Di'ma has told me that these female thieves double up as child-lifter also.'

I had to raise my eyebrows with suitable expression of fear, saying, 'Good Heavens!'

Then I heaved sigh of relief and said, 'Anyway, let those with children bother about it. You don't have a child yet.'

Immediately, Brajabala's lips swelled in anguish. Like a practised bride, she pulled the border of the sari over her head and looked at me with anxiety-filled eyes, saying, 'So what? Don't I have other concerns? Your Dada said they can even lure him away.'

My Dada? Did she mean Prahlad? Must be. Since I had called her Bouthan, he would automatically be my elder brother. How tender was the girl's heart! What unflinching trust! Truly, Prahlad was the only man in her life. It did not matter that he was thin and dark and addicted to ganja. I was hard put to suppress my laughter, seeing her playing the role of a sister-in-law to the hilt, but did not dare to laugh, lest her mood changed.

I was scandalized by Prahlad's warped sense of humour. What rubbish he had fed to his gullible minor wife that the wretched girl was smarting with anxiety?

Outwardly, I declared, 'You don't have to worry. I am there.'

I said so, thrusting my chest forward. In any case, because of a good round of oil-rubbing, my chest was a little puffed up. But it seemed that I did not make much impression on Braja Bouthan. She looked at me contemplatively for a moment, then bit into another ripe jujube and asked, 'Are you married?'

I replied, 'No, why?'

Brajabala said, 'The bachelors have more to fear, don't you know?'

Well, to tell the truth, I knew it quite well. But I was surprised that Braja also knew. The petals of the flower of her youth had not opened up yet. But she was carrying the legacy of all the married Bengali girls. The potential of a future well-blossomed young woman was peeping out of her character. The flower and fruit of life were latent in her eternal feminine nature. Was there any sin in her knowledge of the forbidden fruit? Was there any precociousness? I did not know. But this was the beginning of her life's lesson. It is the misfortune of our society that at this age she could not go to the pathshala. The fundamentals of all our families, from the secretariat of Delhi to the daily wager of the small town, would crumble to dust if Brajabalas were not there.

I assured Braja by saying, 'Are you talking of marriage? I've finished that job long back. That thief woman will not be able to harm me in any way.'

She asked, 'Are you telling the truth?'

I replied with another question, 'Why, did it sound like a lie?'

Braja turned serious, 'Difficult to guess. The modern boys do not marry so early. I guess I have to keep an eye on you. No one knows where the danger lurks.'

Looking at Braja's agonized demeanour, I again felt like laughing out loud. But I did not want to break the spell of this conversation. So, I teased her further, saying, 'Well, are you also not a modern young girl?'

She still had a number of jujubes in the lap of her drape-end. Putting another of them in her mouth, she said, 'So what?' Then lowering her voice one notch, the grave girl shared an information, 'Your Dada is not a good fellow. He suffers from diseases, yet does not give up his addiction. In the fear that he might go further astray, Di'ma has married him off early. After all, he is a man.'

This accusation of 'manhood' would never escape us. The moment you gained some height, your voice broke in adolescence, line of moustache appeared above your lips, the problem would start. The mind would be restless. The desire for acquiring a lady-love would rise in the breast like a storm. That would lead to a series of desperate moves. The army of grandmas, mothers and fathers would raise a hue and cry that the boy was going astray. How to save him? Get a Brajabala and make him walk seven steps with her. From now onwards, Brajbala was a host in herself.

This was not untrue. But truth was conditioned by time and space. Societies evolved. At least, it had done so in case of menfolk. But what about women? Looking at Braja, I was not sure if women's situation had changed much.

I teased her, asking, 'Hope he does not commit other sins.'

The young girl's face lit up in anger. Her head cover slipped off. Her long braids swayed like a pair of snakes. Her eyes dazzled with fire. I felt as if her blue nose ring also dazzled like blue poison. She forgot the jujube in her mouth and hissed, 'Let him try and see.'

I was almost scared at this combative face of Braja. So much of self-respect in such a chit of a girl. So much detestation of the moral sins.

Though my amusement was now mixed with a sense of surprise, still I continued to tease her, saying, 'What if he does it?'

Braja looked at me sharply. Her lips worked in helpless fury, as if they were like the twang of a bow-string. She said, 'Let him do it and see what happens.'

I pushed relentlessly, 'Yet, what if he does it?'

Braja's eyes became blood shot. Light and shade played scintillatingly on her face. Her breath turned heavy and fast. Her lips trembled uncontrollably. Suddenly, the serpent raised her hood. She said, 'I'll leave him.'

Totally taken aback, I asked, 'Where will you go?'

By that time, tears were streaming down the hapless girl's cheeks. With a muffled voice, she said, 'Wherever my eyes take me, whichever way my mind leads me to. But I'll leave, believe me.'

I shrank in shame and remorse. Fie, fie on me. Considering her a minor child, I was just playing with her. I did not know I had hurt the emotion of a guileless girl. I would never offer any defence of child marriage. But although the flower of youth had not yet blossomed in her body, love had sprouted in her mind. Who could deny that the girl had loved. That dark, skinny, addicted Prahlad had become the king of her heart. That is why there was so much anger, so much pain, so much tears.

I cursed myself and quickly said, 'Good heavens! Why are you crying? I was just kidding. Can anyone cheat such a beautiful wife like you?'

Braja cast me a quick tear-filled glance. Then she averted her face and wiped her tears. The cloud had cleared. Wind had started blowing. There was a sweet smile on her face. A bit of embarrassment too.

I tried to divert her mind and said, 'Well, what has brought you to Kumbh-mela in the first place?'

She replied in a clear tone, 'I came for him.'

For Prahlad? I asked again, 'But why?'

Braja replied, 'Di'ma wanted it.'

I persisted, 'Why did she want it?'

Braja replied exasperatedly, 'You ask too many "why's". Di'ma said that if he visits the Kumbh and takes a bath in the Triveni, all his sicknesses will be cured and…'

'And?'

'And his mind will be purified. He will no longer think of bad things.'

Looking at Brajabala's serious face, I realized that she believed in every word she said. True, our society was still full of a thousand superstitions. We are stuck in a stagnant pool of water with all our desires and ambitions.

And yet, I could not pooh-pooh Brajabala's faith. She was the propitious woman of all ages. Very ordinary and yet extraordinary in joys and sorrows, in want and desire. I remembered Rabindranath Tagore's message on his last birth anniversary. He said, 'It is a sin to lose faith in humanity.'

I had never lost it. Hence, I discovered in Braja another specimen of great human spectacle.

For a moment, my mind was replete with emotion. The strength of Braja's character had stunned me. I came in search of nectar. In lieu, I found Brajabala in the tent. Young bride. Talked in a precocious tone. I was free of any superstition. Though my urban mind was a trained reformist, this young girl flooded my mind with all her otherwise regressive outlook. I discovered a new value system—of love and faith.

Suddenly, from behind the tent, the now-familiar strident voice was heard, 'Hey, Braja, the wretched girl! Where have you vanished?'

It was obvious that the cooking space was just behind the tent. The clattering sound of the utensils could be heard.

Braja jumped up instantly and replied, 'I'm here, Didima. What do you need?'

'Where is the bottle of oil?'

Braja started. In a scared tone, she whispered, 'Oh, my God!'

My condition was no better. The whole body was glistening with oil. If she came this way, I would be caught red-handed.

Although Braja was scared, a mischievous smile was playing on her lips. She shouted back, 'The bottle of oil? I've no idea, Di'ma!

Saying so, she burst into a muffled laughter and told me, 'Run, run to the bathing space.'

She picked up the bottle of oil like a hawk picks up its prey and hid it somewhere inside her oversized sari. Then she looked at me and quickly gauged that I did not know the way to the bathing space.

Taking pity on me, she said in a conspiratorial tone, 'Okay. Follow me. When we reach the spot, you vanish inside. I will keep going.'

I could clearly see that for the child-bride this whole affair was a game. The lonely girl had found a playmate in me.

So be it. I followed her. The ashram courtyard was more or less empty. All the morning programmes were over. Reaching the tube-well, I found that women surrounded it like bees around a hive. I had no other way but to patiently wait with the gamcha covering my torso. The other alternative was to run to the river.

On the other side, Didima's raucous voice could still be heard, 'The bottle was lying here only. My God, this place is infested with thieves. Someday they may even take away our clothes.'

I smiled to myself. How was that possible? The task of stealing the clothes of the cowherd girls was the monopoly of only one person—Lord Krishna.

But before I could enjoy my own sense of humour, I again heard the suspicious voice, 'Do you have any idea where the bottle could be, Braja?'

I shrank in fear. If Braja was caught, I would also be caught.

Braja's innocent reply was, 'No, Di'ma. But let me search it out.'

Didima said, 'Where else will you search? My plan to fry a few *bodis* has to be given up. What a dangerous place, dear. These sinners do not even have the fear of God. This is a pilgrimage, a place of living God. But let me also curse, 'The one who has taken it…'

Braja quickly interrupted, 'Got it, Di'ma.' …'Where did you find it?' …'Just behind the oven?' …'But I could not see it there?'

How would you? I thought. You did not know that Braja was a magician.

Now, the women around the tube-well were also following the episode. A lady with a rather large shape joined the issue in a grating tone, 'The wretched woman has a raucous voice. Herself is devoid of eyesight. And she was accusing everyone as thief.'

Nobody responded. Perhaps the immediate business with water was more engaging. Maybe, they buried the issue presently to discuss it threadbare in leisure time.

But the widow with the huge mass was not one to let go of such an opportunity. She made a strange face and declared, 'If she had implicated me, I would have thrashed her face on the stone.'

Having declared war in this manner, she looked around to see if she had made the desired impact on anyone.

One woman was looking at her. A middle-aged married woman. She responded in a quiet voice, 'She has not talked to you at all. Why are you shouting? And yes, there are thieves all around here. So, what she said is nothing wrong.'

That was just the spark the widow needed to explode. The large woman shouted back, 'How do you say so? Your oil bottle was lying behind the oven and you were cursing the whole world. This is like a pickpocket giving witness in favour of a petty thief.'

The situation was going beyond control. It seemed I would be required to go to Ganga after all.

At that point, a young voice called out, 'Hey, Khana Aunty, your brinjals are getting overfried.'

'Overfried? Oh, God.' Saying so, Khana Aunty hastily entered below the tube-well. Quite a few were pushed aside. But no one dared protest. I realized that Khana Aunty had already established her credentials in the ashram as someone not to be toyed with.

Didima was a great cook. In the sandy expanse of the Kumbh-mela, I never expected such wonderful vegetable curry of cabbage and *bodi*. If the pilgrimage provided such food, I was ready to stay here for the whole year.

A little rest was called for after such a sumptuous lunch. But since I had not had much sleep last night, the little rest for me turned into a few hours' sleep. When I woke up, it was dark all around. There was no one in the tent. Raising the screen, I found a sea of humanity in the ashram courtyard. A host of men, women and children. Light was flooding all around. Different colours of garments had made the ashram resplendent. The atmosphere was charged with conversations, laughter and song.

I felt I had missed out a lot. I got up and quickly got dressed. A chill was gradually descending on the Kumbh-mela. Going out, I was immediately struck by a spark of light. That light was the beauty of a woman. I never knew that a woman could be so glamorously attractive.

Somebody whispered in my ear, 'Here comes Ramjidasi.' There was a commotion all around. Everyone wanted to have a good look at her. I stood transfixed with a sense of wonder and disbelief. There was no time to think how that beauty was. Lines of a song automatically formed in my lips:

As if the blossomed lamp was lit up towards the azure sky...

I looked at the sky. My mystery-seeker mind often tried to fathom what was there beyond the blue sky. Looking at Ramjidasi, I felt as if my imagination had at last been able to uncover the blue lid of the sky. Such beauty! That too in a *brahmacharini*!

I had read that the extraordinary beauty of women had brought down mighty empires. Had burnt down golden thrones and tall towers. Had killed thousands of soldiers! Forget foreign land. The saga of Queen Padmini in our own country came back to my mind.

Were those beauteous women like her? Or even more beautiful? I would not know. I was totally absorbed in the living example in front of me. The kotwal mentioned that she was a daughter of Himachal. But she looked like the peak of the snow-covered Kanchanjhenga, dazzling under the first rays of the sun.

I would rather refrain from describing her beauty. But what kind of ascetic was she! She was clad in a fine white muslin sari, with borders of delicate silver colour. She had worn it in modern fashion with the border folded on her shoulder. There was no ornament on her body. But her long braid of thick black hair was coiling down her back like a serpent. Age? Not possible to guess, at least not by a man.

Her gait did not have the vanity of a beautiful woman. But her eyes were alert and fickle. Her ruddy lips had a suppressed smile. Her huge pair of eyes were sparkling with a strange dark light.

A lot of men and women were trailing her. A man was walking beside her. He was clad in a dazzling attire. A white turban decorated his head. He was carrying a sarod in his hand.

Ramjidasi climbed up the stage and bowed down before the Mohanta. The Mohanta was wearing just a loincloth. His naked torso was smeared with ash. His eyes were red. He did not even look at Ramjidasi. Just raised his hand towards the sky in a gesture of benediction. The *brahmachari* sat on one side of the stage.

The moon had risen on the sky. Not a rounded one, but like a worn out dish. There was a light fog all around. It looked the whole mela was covered in a mist. To enhance the mystery further, dew drops were shining on the white sand.

The whole mela was full of noise—of microphones and of the crowd. There were lights of different hues all around, making it look like a spectacle. Occasionally, I thought I was passing the night in a modern city. Advertisement of different wares in bright colours would remind you of the commercial area of a city. And the aristocratic Hudson and

Austin cars moving with dignified horns further enhanced this illusion.

A few cars raised a storm of sand and stopped at our ashram gate. Well-dressed men and women came down and entered the ashram. A lady was trying to enter with her chained pet dog. But the sanyasi guard stopped her. 'Dogs are not allowed, Mataji.' She frowned. What was the way out then? She must attend the programme. Finally, she locked the dog in the car and entered the ashram.

Young men in suits were standing on one side with hands in their pockets. There was surprise and curiosity in their eyes. Looking at Ramjidasi, they were commenting in a low tone and elbowing each other in secret fun and joke.

On the other side, trouble was brewing at the women's quarter. The colourful dupattas of the Punjabi women were dominating the scene. They were stronger and louder in reposte too. The quarrel was between two languages unknown to each other, Punjabi and Bengali.

Somebody said, 'My, my, where do I move further? What is this woman saying?'

A woman's voice barked in protest. I also did not understand the language. But one could guess that the following exchanges were about whose forefathers owned the space here or for that matter whether the whole Kumbh-mela was bought by so and so's father or husband.

Suddenly, I heard a familiar voice. It was the large widow from the bathing area. She commented, 'What a loud-mouthed woman! The Punjabi lady who lives near our house is not so quarrelsome.' The statement suggested a hint of retreat.

The microphone announced, 'This is a place of living God. O mothers, you are serving God for these few days. Please do not quarrel here. God will be displeased. Now Ramjidasi Brahmacharini will sing to you the glory of Godhead Ram.'

The words were uttered in a mixed language. Hindi was the base, but there were Bengali words also punched in between.

The quarrelsome voices fell somewhat silent. The tanpura started tuning. Ramjidasi was sitting with folded palms. Her eyes were closed. I did not know what was there in that face. But it seemed to have lighted the entire stage. I must admit that it was the light of Ramjidasi's stunning beauty. That beauty was not soft like cold water. You were not beckoned here to feel refreshed by taking a dip in the still deep water. It was like an unbearable flame, burning bright like a fireplace. The audience were mesmerized by this great beauty. They were looking at her unblinkingly and listening to her song with rapt attention.

My plight was no better. She appeared to me as wrapped in mystery like the caves of Himachal, her birthplace. I moved a little farther from the crowd. It would give me a better view and I could enjoy her beauty in seclusion. As I neared the fence, I saw a few dark shapes sitting by the fence, covered in torn clothes and tattered blankets. Their eyes were fixed on the stage. Some were smoking ganja. A few smoldering chillums were moving from hand to hand. In Panchugopal's language, *saptami*. As my eyes got accustomed to the darkness, I could see ashes smeared on their faces and bodies. That would mean that these were all sadhus.

Someone was passing by in hurry. We collided. I saw it was the kotwal. I called, 'Kotwalji, sadhuji!'

He turned, 'Who is that? O you! But why here? Go to the front row.'

I replied, 'No, it is better from afar.'

The kotwal glanced at the stage once, briefly; then turned his face. Under that magical moonlight, I fancied I saw a softening in his face. He said rather seriously, 'All right. See from a distance. One can see better from a distance.'

As he made to move, I asked, 'Where are you rushing to?'

This time, the kotwal smiled and said, 'That sorceress is roaming about. Attempted to enter the ashram twice, but failed. She has gone on that side of the fence. Let me see if I can apprehend her.'

I started walking with him and asked, 'Sorceress? Who are you talking about?'

The kotwal replied, 'Oh, you are not aware of the goings-on? She is the most dreaded of the women thieves' gang. Once or twice, the police has caught her, but I don't know how she manages to escape each time.'

True, I had heard something like this from Brajabala also. Looking in front of me, I saw thousands of men and women proceeding by the fence from east to west and north to south. How would the female thief break the fence in the midst of such crowd and enter the ashram. After all, she was not a magician!

When I shared my thought with the kotwal, he simply said, 'It is among the crowd that she operates better. More the crowd, higher are her chances.'

Reaching the western fence, the kotwal suddenly halted. The crowd was a little thinner on this side. He gazed at the crowd and drew my attention to a particular direction.

'Look, a figure is running towards the Ganga. Have you seen her?'

I could not see anything immediately. But once my eyesight got accustomed to the crowd, I noticed a running figure, decidedly feminine, floating up among the crowd from time to time. The border of her sari was fluttering in the wind.

The kotwal said, 'Whenever she spies someone she knows, she flees. But you can never be sure of her flight. The very next moment you can find her tiptoeing back towards the camp in the darkness around the bank of Jhusi. She must have been a leopard in her previous birth.'

I was suitably impressed. A thief, that too a woman. And if you believed Brajabala, a young and beautiful woman thief. I smelt a mystery here.

At that moment, I heard a voice on the microphone and looked back. Ramjidasi had opened her eyes. Tuning her voice with the tanpura, she was now just chanting—'Ram Ram Ram Ram, Ram Ram Ram Ram.' For a few moments,

Ramjidasi sang the name alone. It was plain and simple chanting without any subtle musical manouevre. A little later, a few men and two more women joined her in the chanting. Who were these people? I turned to ask the kotwal and found to my amazement that he had vanished without even taking leave.

A little farther, a person was standing alone by the bamboo fence. Thinking that he might be the kotwal, I went near him. No, it was a different sadhu. His eyes were intensely focused on the stage. In the dim light, I could only guess that he was fair. His face was covered in curling beard and mustache. Even in this biting cold, he was wearing only a thin saffron cotton dhoti. His hair cascaded down on his shoulder. There was no attempt at matting. He was wearing a rosary of rudraksha around his neck.

I felt that it was not only his eyes that focused on the stage, but his mind too. At first, he did not even notice that I was standing near him. Realizing my mistake, I turned to leave. That was when he suddenly became alive to the circumstances and called back in chaste Hindi, 'Babuji, were you looking for something?'

I was slightly embarrassed. I should not have ogled like that.

I said haltingly, 'I was looking for someone. Thought you were him.'

I thought the matter would rest there. But the sadhu laughed out loudly. There was a suppressed excitement in his laughter. An excitement akin to madness.

He commented, not without trepidation, 'You thought I was *him*. Ha ha ha. Where is *he*? How can you find *him* here?'

Again the same words. The same sentiment. I was hearing it for the third time in a day.

'You are looking for *him*, Babuji. I am also looking for *him*. Searching through the world. Spent a whole life in this search. And yet, no scent of *him*.'

There was no reply to such utterances. I made to go.

But he again laughed and asked quite normally, 'Whom were you exactly looking for, Babuji?'

I said, 'The kotwalji of this ashram.'

'Ramananda-ji? He just walked down this side.'

I was surprised, 'Who is Ramananda-ji?'

'Why, the kotwal of this ashram.'

'You know him?'

'Of course I do. For many years.' The sadhu again started laughing in suppressed tone.

I persisted, 'Do you belong to this ashram?'

The sadhu said, 'No.' And then hurriedly added, 'Look, look, Rukmini is dancing.'

I looked back. Ramjidasi had now climbed down the stage and tied the border of her sari around her waist. On the stage, three young boys were sitting near the Mohanta. Two of them were dressed as warriors with bows and arrows. One was dressed like a queen.

I asked, 'Who are these people?'

The sadhu laughed. There was some fun and even derision in his laughter.

He said, 'They are Ram, Lakshman and Sita. A kirtan party has brought them all dressed up. Rukmini would dance now. Have you heard of Mirabai, Babuji? A devotee of Lord Krishna. Nay, you can say Krishna-intoxicated. Queen Mirabai's body turned to jelly if someone uttered the name of Kishen Kanhaiya in front of her. This Ramjidasi is also mad in love of Ram. Wherever she goes, the kirtan party comes there with living images of Ram-Sita. Otherwise, Ramjidasi would constantly search for him through her dance. She becomes crazy, at times laughing, at times crying, sometimes even fainting.

I asked, 'You mentioned Rukmini? Who is she?'

'What do I call her then? Muniabai?

'Who is Muniabai?'

'It was the earlier name of Ramjidasi. But Muniabai died long back.'

I was curious. Under the foggy moonlight, I could smell a mysterious tale of the past in the sadhu's utterances. But before I could make any further query, the sarod and the tabla started playing the dancing number. Ramjidasi started singing,

Kaun bon pahunche sakhi do peyara, do peyara
Yakey bhajan meowa mithai
Tey koyse banafal karat ahara.

She was simultaneously dancing. I was surprised to notice that her dance movements, the mudras of her palms and fingers, the nimble movements of her feet—these were not that of an untrained rustic. In her every step, the ankle bells rang out a different sound. It was the display of great talent. My heart swelled up in the rhythm of her dance. I forgot that I was standing on a sand-band in an ashram. I felt I was transported to an auditorium holding a classical dance recital.

With each movement of her dance, Ramjidasi's beauty became more dazzling. Earlier, it was amber covered with ash. Now the ash had flown away and the amber had turned a cinder. The glamour of her beauty turned bewitching. She was wearing a makhmal sari in a modern fashion. Each fold of that sari gave out a promise of mystery. The braid of her hair was as if hissing like a moving cobra on her back.

Yakey achowan Saraju Gangajal
Tey koyse peot jangal jal khara.

And then came the piteous entreaty, '*Kaho, kaho meri raja*.' The language of the song sounded like a dialect. I could not decipher the meaning of all that. It seemed, the forest-dweller Ram was being asked, 'You are a prince. Your daily food was *mewa mithai*. But now how are you eating wild fruits? You used to drink pure water of the Ganga. But, hey Ram, how do you now drink the water of the jungle? Your feet were always on soft bed, now how do you roam in forests and hills? O Ram, you have accepted this grief on your own accord. But I find it unbearable.'

Rukminidasi had created a spell in the congregation. Everyone present was deeply immersed in the sentiment of bhakti, the devotion. People were initially charmed by her physical beauty, but now they are swayed by her invocation of devotion to the Godhead.

The sadhu standing next to me said, 'Ulara'.

I asked, 'What is Ulara?'

'That's the name of this song, Babuji. The maidens and housewives of this land sing this song during festivals.' I noticed that even the sadhuji was also intensely moved by the song.

By now, it was dance all out on the stage. Ramjidasi was dancing like a woman possessed. In rhythm with her steps, sarod was playing its tune, tabla was giving out its *bol*s, tanpura was maintaining the background music. Beyond the stage, there was the endless blue sky and the everflowing river. A perfect natural scenario for a perfect musical soiree.

Ramjidasi's dance was not bereft of drama. A lot of abhinaya was on display. Now she was bubbling with joy and smile; the next moment her face was contorted in agony and pangs of separation. Sometimes, she was acting the coy lover; at other times, the coquette to the core; sometimes, she was sending flirty signals with her eyes; at other times, she was bowing down with devotion. At times, only the fluidity of her body movement was silently expressing what was going on in her mind.

Although I was deeply engrossed in this spectacle, I did not forget the sadhuji. An intense curiosity attracted me towards him like a magnet. The names Rukmini and Muniabai had intrigued me.

Suddenly, the sadhu laughed and said, 'The woman, at whose doors once millionaires queued up to enjoy dance performances, is today serving God by travelling from fair to fair.'

I turned towards him and asked, 'Millionaires visited to see this Ramjidasi's dance?'

The sanyasi smiled disapprovingly and said, 'Not Ramjidasi, Babuji. I was talking of Muniabai of Lucknow, who was matchless in beauty throughout Delhi and Lucknow. When honey gathers in a flower, the bee gets to know about it, because he is the *rasika*, the connoisseur. They used to come from Calcutta, Bombay and other places. A few could get to see her. Many returned disappointed. For, she was not the kind of *baiji* who would please her lover with sidelong glances, false laughter and seductive love songs. No, Babuji. Muniabai was different.'

While saying this, sadhuji's expression underwent some change. That derisive laughter was replaced by a piteous expression. His gaze was fixed at the horizon as if he was viewing a different cosmic game being played on a different stage. He mused something in his rustic Hindi, part of which I understood, part I did not.

'Babuji, you must admit that God is showing us many *leela*s, his whimsical play. He has shown us one game through Muniabai's life. Muniabai enjoyed the attention of the high and mighty, sitting on a golden bed, so to say. But in her heart, she was nurturing the idol of Raghunandan.'

Suddenly, he called out, 'Raghunandan! O the great sage, O Guru, I bow to your feet.'

I asked, 'Who is Raghunandan?'

He replied, 'A great sanyasi, Babuji. Sanyasis are not defined just by matted hair, ash-smeared body and loud uttering of 'Byom! Byom!' The sanyasi, Raghunandan, was love incarnate. Whoever has heard him speak has experienced ecstasy. One would feel as if a blessed god intoxicated acharya from the past has come and stood before you. His shadow fell on the heart of Muniabai also. If your life is touched by that grace, there is no getting away from it. Even if you plunge into fire, it would survive in your ash, in your soul. Ha ha ha… Of what use are the huge mansion of Lucknow, the golden bedstead, the gems and jewels, when Raghunandan's shadow has fallen on you? Babuji, the crazy lechers would pour bottles of wine on Muniabai's naked body. That wine would flow down her legs. The louts would lap it up from her legs like greedy dogs. These were not human beings, but beasts. And among these beasts, the *baiji* would flirt and giggle, and sing and dance. Then suddenly, she would start acting like a woman possessed, shouting, throwing things, tearing away the screens. Seeing that fierce look, the lascivious beasts would run away. That is why she was also called the 'crazy *baiji*' in Lucknow. Her sin was embedded in her beauty. An intense light was hidden under her sin. When that light flared up, she had to be mad. For it is then Raghunandan used to come, take her in his embrace, caress her, love her. And then one day—'

Suddenly, the sadhu stopped. As if he had remembered something urgent, he spoke in a different trajectory, 'But Babuji, what was the ultimate gain? Look at Ramjidasi, put your hands on your chest and tell the truth. What do you see? Her physical beauty. Everyone here is bewitched by her dazzling charm. Don't you feel that a colourful bird is stirring in your mind? That is the bird of desire. People run to pilgrimages in search of piety. But Nature takes her revenge through this mysterious woman. But let me stop here. People will laugh at me if they hear my blabbering.'

The sadhu stopped. But my mind did not. I was staring at Ramjidasi's devastating figure. She stood motionless, with her palms folded, eyes closed. All the singers on the stage had started singing a kirtan.

Ramjidasi and Muniabai. Muniabai and Raghunandan. An intriguing tale was lurking from behind the past. I felt as if the whole Kumbh-mela was enveloped by this mysterious tale.

I eagerly asked, 'Tell me the rest of Muniabai's story, sadhuji.'

But the sadhu pulled down the shutters, saying, 'These are the secrets of a *sanyasini*'s past. A householder is not supposed to know it. Forgive me.'

As he made to leave, I entreated, 'I want to hear unless there is any serious objection.'

The sadhu gave me a searching look. As if he was trying to gauge the genuineness of my curiosity. Then he said, 'You can hear the rest of the story from the kotwal of your ashram.'

Maybe, Ramanandan-ji would tell me. But one was never sure of the mood of these sanyasis.

I acted like a blackguard. Taking a step nearer to the sadhu, I said, 'If you don't mind, I would like to hear it from you.'

'Why do you want to hear it? This is the love story of a sansyasin. You may feel repulsed.'

Possible. Still I said, 'Love story of a sanyasin is rare. This is precisely why I want to hear it.'

The sadhu smiled. Then signaling me to follow him, he started walking towards the gate of the ashram. Once again I looked at Ramjidasi. A real flame for the moths to singé. The entire congregation was staring at her spellbound.

We pushed our way through the thick crowd at the gate. Outside also, there were thousands of people, but because of the endless space, it looked sparse. The sadhu proceeded towards the south-east corner of the Sangam, where the river Saraswati was believed to have gone underground. This part was not well lit. But there was moon in the sky. Although it was severely cold, one could still see the autumn blue in the sky of Uttar Pradesh. There were chickpea fields on the elevated Jhusi land.

The more we advanced, deeper became the sand. Our feet started sinking beneath it.

The sadhu turned towards me and spoke in a very soft voice, 'Have you never heard of a sanyasi's love story?

Normally, a sanyasi's love is in his meditation and dharma. In dharma and karma. His love says, 'Oh Goddess, the source of my inspiration, oh beloved, oh possessor of the beautiful face, please govern the five senses of the sanyasi. But there is a lot of rituals, a lot of efforts in this love. Secret do's beyond the ambit of the domestic life. The common people are scared of these processes... Sit down, Babuji. Let me tell you a secret ritual of the sanyasis.'

We sat down on the sand, ignoring the fact that it was wet with dew. Unlike us, these sadhus were totally oblivious of the physical discomfiture.

He said, 'Some ritual practices must have a female counterpart. You are a Bengali. In your land, this practice was more prevalent. Look at your Krishna-devotee Chandidas. He sang of Lord Krishna's *leela*, but he had a washerwoman as his muse, Rami. The Buddhist tantrics selected five types of women for such sadhana—a Brahmin woman, a *chandal* woman, a courtesan, a *dom* woman and a washerwoman. In the Brahmanya tantra, four more types were added—prostitute, *kapali*, barber woman and cowherd girl. In some tantra practices, there are sixty-four castes of women, even the *yavani* (the Muslim or the Christian) is not excluded.'

At this point, the sadhu looked at my face, perhaps to gauge if I was following the discourse. But I have heard these details a number of times. So, I was not particularly surprised or impressed. I wanted to listen to Raghunandan's story.

But the sadhu continued, 'There is not much of a difference between a sanyasi and an *avadhut*. They often worship a flame, desiring the appearance of Devi Balasundari. A lamp is lighted with ghee and camphor. Around it, Lord Brahma, Goddess Kali, Lord Vishnu, Lord Hanuman and the Bhairav are kept as witnesses. The ingredients of this worship are *prathama, dwitiya, tritiya, moti* and *chakra*. Do you understand, Babuji? It means wine, meat, fish, rice and puri. These are key elements. There are *saptami* and *shashthi* also, ganja and tobacco. This is the way to enter the path of flame. One who enters, is to perform a final ritual. He has to keep the Navaratra fast in the month of Chaitra (usually mid-March to mid-April). Then he is to sit in a round ring with fellow sanyasis in a secret place and copulate with a woman. This physical congress is the climax of the secret ritual, without which you cannot attain the power. There is a lot of esoteric arguments in it, all of which you won't understand, Babuji.'

I did not need to understand either. I had heard about these practices, but they left me cold. We are ordinary social beings. We know the simple meaning of sadhana (meditation), *tapasya* (ascetic discipline) and bhakti (devotion). Then why these complications?

But I did not protest. I simply asked, 'What happened to Raghunandan?'

The sadhu replied, 'I told you all this just as a background to Raghunandan and Rukmini's story. Like Rukmini, Raghunandan was also extremely handsome. He was born in a Brahmin family in this Allahabad. He looked like Lord Shiva himself. Not only in beauty, but in virtue also. If he looked at your eyes or touched you, you would have goosebumps on your body. The sadhus of the Niranjani Akhra used to taunt him. They would say, "You are not meant to be a sanyasi. Shave off your beard and moustache and go to Navadwip wearing a sari." But, Raghunandan grew so wise and learned that the same sadhus, being defeated by him in shastra discourses, would dig the earth with their tridents in impotent fury. This Raghunandan met Rukmini in Hardwar. He was then preparing to hold the Navaratra fast after completing the initiation into the path of flame.'

I felt as if I was listening to an incident of the hoary past. Not of India that I knew. But an India of the Hindu past.

I could not resist interfering, 'When did all this take place? How long ago?'

The sadhu said, 'Well, must be around fifteen–sixteen years ago.'

Surprised, I asked again, 'Then what's the age of Ramjidasi?'

He laughed and counter-questioned, 'What's your guess, Babuji?'

For me, it was impossible to guess the age of a woman. Still I said, 'Maybe twenty-five–twenty-six years.'

The sadhu laughed and said triumphantly, 'Add a good ten more years, Babuji.'

I was now completely flummoxed. I could see that blemishless face and that hourglass figure in my mind's eyes. Who could have thought that she was a thirty-five-year-old woman?

The sadhu reminisced, 'The day on which she came to our ashram, as if a hundred flowers blossomed in our empty garden. She was accompanied by her husband. Simple village folk. It was the month of Chaitra. Usually, Hardwar is crowded during this time. The pilgrims to Kedarnath-Badrinath have started pouring in. Water from melted snow was cascading down in various spots. With the Mohanta's permission, Rukmini's husband started cooking a meal in the ashram. They had come from further north. And was going for a darshan of Badrinarayan. There was a secret cave behind the ashram. It was there that the arrangement for the observation of Navaratra was made. Many from the ashram were busy there. A few devotees had also come with their consorts to witness the ritual. Everything was being done under a screen of secrecy.'

The sadhu remained silent for a few moments and then laughed out, 'Raghunandan was quite a strange fellow. He would repeatedly come out of the secret rendezvous and sit with the Mohanta. Every time he caught my eyes, he smiled. That was not the beatific smile of a sanyasi, but the lusty smile of a normal young man. It smacked of secret love. But there was a frown of deep thought also on Raghunandan's face. I was the kotwal of the ashram then. Suddenly, Raghunandan came to me and declared, "Kotwalji, I am unable to attend the *chakra* at night." I was stunned. I stared at him for a few moments. He was looking extremely handsome that day. He had put on a new saffron robe upto his knee. A garland of thorn apple flowers adorned his neck. Another rosary of rudraksh inlaid with coral was there. His matted hair was also bound with a garland of coral. His golden complexion covered by ash was looking like smoldering amber. There was red sandalwood paste on his forehead, chest and throat. Shiva incarnate!'

'Raghunandan was rather casual in his approach to everything. That's why he could not become the Mohanta. In a *math*, the Mohanta is usually elected by the sanyasins. They would always prefer one who could carry everyone else along. Such correct and diplomatic conduct was beyond Raghunandan. But he was the wisest among us. It is from him that we learnt the history of religion. His theological knowledge was boundless. So, hearing his decision about the Navaratri *chakra*, I was dumbfounded.

I could only blurt out, "Why?"

He coolly replied, "Not finding enough enthusiasm from within."

I advised, "Once you sit down at the circle (*chakra*), you will find the enthusiasm."

He countered, "That won't be fair. When the doors of my heart are closed, God will not be happy with my service."

At that point, Rukmini came and stood before us. She folded her palms and looked up at Raghunandan. Raghunandan blessed her by saying, "Let Lord Narayana give you a long life."

As I have told you earlier, Babuji, Rukmini's advent would as if make the flowers bloom. Everyone had grown fond of her not only because of her stunning appearance, but also for her gentle voice and pure laughter. She was like a mountain spring, always restless, always playful. But she turned totally still and mute on seeing Raghunandan. There was the sparkle of a different light in her eyes. She was not ashamed at her conduct, but just stood there with her palms folded. Her hair was flowing in the wind. Babuji, at that moment I saw the flicker of the same light in Raghunandan's eyes. I knew it was sinful on the part of a sanyasi to be charmed by a woman's beauty. But I felt as if I was witnessing Shiva and Parvati in front of me.

I had work to do. The sanyasins of other ashrams who were interested in the path of flame needed to be informed of the timings and all. When I returned, dusk had already fallen. Mohanta-ji had already sat down for his evening meditation. There was a suppressed excitement on the faces of a few of the sanyasins of the *akhra*. This always happened on the Navaratra nights. None of them was a real *sadhak*. The prospect of a momentary pleasure still excited them.

I proceeded towards the secret cave to see what Raghunandan was doing. At first sight, I thought the cave was deserted. Then I noticed two figures in deep embrace against the dark stone. Raghunandan did not say anything. But Rukmini laughed. She was wearing a saffron robe. Babuji, that was the moment when I realized how charming she was. The saffron had as if enhanced the impact of her dazzling beauty. Her laughter brought me back to reality. I asked feebly, "What do you want?"

Rukmini replied, “We shall join the *chakra* for the Navaratra ritual.”

She needed not say anything more. I understood that Raghunandan had come to some terms with her.

By that time, two lamps had already been lit on two sides of the room. One was for Mahadev, the other far Mahakali. All the participant sanyasins arrived. Also the saffron-clad women, the *bhairavis*. The tantrik rituals continued for a long time. At the end, each participating sanyasi had union with one or the other *bhairavis*. Rukmini went and stood in front of Raghunandan. Raghunandan took her as his Shiva-Shakti consort.

For the next two days, I did not see Raghunandan, nor Rukmini, nor her husband even. Usually, after the Navaratra rituals, the discipline in the *akhra* turned a little slack. There were apparent irregularities all around.

On the third day, I found Raghunandan returning from a bath in the Ganga. But he was not his former self. That smiling wise sanyasi was gone. This was an ecstatic young man who, in reply to my formal greeting “Om Namoh Narayana”, held my hands and said in a tremulous tone, “Mahavir bhai!” This mode of address sounded rather odd to me.

I asked, “What happened?”

He replied, “I have acquired a new wisdom.”

I was immediately relieved. He must have received a new light during the Jyotimarg sadhana the other night.

I eagerly asked, “What kind of wisdom?”

Raghunandan replied, “I don’t know really.”

Babuji, I noticed that his eyes were full of tears, but his mouth had a blissful smile. His look was dreamy, and distant. Suddenly he was jolted back to attention and said, "Do you hear?"

"What?"

"The sweet twittering of the birds."

"Yes, but that I hear every day."

He said, "Therein lies the joy. Great joy! You hear it always? But I have not listened to it so far. I have not noticed the vast sky. The wind had never fanned my body this crazily earlier. Whatever is simple is beautiful. Instead of enjoying all this, we are stuck in the *akhra* with ash on our body. We bragged our knowledge. What is knowledge, Mahavir Bhai? Intelligence? No, it's a mistake. If there is no rasa, ecstasy in the heart, flower does not blossom in the head. It is that flower in the head which is wisdom. Its root is in the heart. So long my heart was blind. But now it has got sight. I realized that we were blindly following customs, and chanting mantras. What is mantra? Can it be taught? It should spontaneously come out of one's heart. When Surdas roams the streets singing, it is that song which is his mantra. This is the only way we can serve God. Everything else is a lie. And to follow that path you have to see the manifest God in everything."

I was completely flustered, "What are you saying, Raghunandan?"

He replied, "I am telling the truth. You are my God. You, and this earth, this wind, water, that singing bird, that sky. His appearance is reflected in all this. I have missed it so long."

I was exasperated. I said, "You are a renunciator, with full initiation into the *sanyas* dharma. You are an *akhra*-dweller *avadhut*. Do you understand the meaning of what you are saying?"

Raghunandan was adamant, "I am telling you the truth, brother. Forget seven Saptaguru, seven preceptors. You are my guru, this Nature is my guru, Rukmini is my guru. Whatever is beautiful, whatever is endless, is my guru. I don't know where it begins. I don't know where it ends."

After a few moment's silence, he again said, "Mahavir bhai, before looking for Godhead, moksha and nirvana, you have to look at yourself. What do I know about myself? The darkness of one's mind is fathomless. Suddenly, I realized that I had been living in Hardwar for so many years, but I do not even know anything about its trees and stones. Never watched them closely. I have thought of every other human being as corrupt and licentious. Oh, forgive me, forgive me, you all."'

By now, I was beyond all surprise. Was I listening to a sanyasi who went through rigorous intellectual discipline or a sufi saint or a God-intoxicated *baul*?

By now, the moon had risen farther up. Occasional flakes of clouds were passing by, momentarily obliterating her. Their movement was from north to south, from the Himalayas to the ocean. Shadows of cloud had fallen on the sand-bed also. The cold had turned more severe. Yet the crowd was steadily increasing. And the concomitant noise.

Mahavir again started speaking, 'Babuji, as Raghunandan went away, I had evil thoughts coming. Was it all genuine realization or had he been trapped by the charm of Rukmini? I forgot the temporary impact his moving words had had on me. As I recollected them, I felt as if they were all paean to that bewitching beauty. Under her devastating influence, he must have lost his wits.'

'On reaching the ashram, I found Rukmini standing there, clad in her normal sari. The saffron was gone, but her great beauty was intact. However, I did not see her husband.

The Mohanta was passing by. He called her and asked, "Aren't you going for the darshan of Badrinath?"

Rukmini laughed with her whole body, as if it was a very funny question. Then she said, "No, father. I would serve Him staying here. Please allow me to stay in your ashram. I will worship Him from here."

Such a request was not unusual. Many hapless women had stayed lifelong in the ashram and offered their labour of love and devotion. But where to keep this burning amber?

The Mohanta again asked, "Where is your husband?"

She replied, "No idea. I haven't seen him for some time."

The opinion was divided among the sanyasins about Rukmini's stay in the ashram. Some said, she might be allowed to stay. Others vehemently objected, saying that she would be a distraction. As no conclusion could be reached, the status quo continued. Rukmini stayed in the ashram.

Nobody uttered a word of suspicion, but everyone kept a close eye on Raghunandan's movements. The idea was to catch them red-handed. But Raghunandan did not make any such move. He was a different man. Not that he cut his matted hair or beard and nor did he stop smearing ash on his body and forehead. But his heart was not there in the worship or rituals. Like *baul* saints, he would laugh out absentmindedly and roam about singing full-throated. All the songs were his own instant compositions. Rukmini swept the courtyard of the *akhra*, mopped the rooms and corridors, drew water from the well and ate prasad. On many occasions, I followed Raghunandan to see if they had a rendeavous. But he would go and sit in a solitary place and start singing:

The day my wings will catch wind
I'll fly in search of you.
When will I sit on your hilltop
And will quench my thirst dipping the lips in the flowing cloud
I will whisper your tale to the people in your world.

People would often gather to listen to his songs. Those who had known him earlier would wonder how such a vastly learned man had turned into a lost soul.

I would often marvel at this dramatic opening up of the fountain of music in him. Who put around his neck this garland of songs? When I sat down for the evening meditation, I would repeatedly see the face of Raghunandan before me. I would hear him singing:

A flower called Brahman has blossomed,

Its fragrance has intoxicated me,
There is fire in the beauty of that flower,
Yet my eyes did not burn
It only lighted a lamp in my blind heart.

Babuji, when Rukmini and Raghunandan met, they would only exchange formal greetings. But Rukmini would become eager and restless. In her desire to be with Raghu, she would often run after him, forgetting that people's tongues would wag. But when Raghunandan smiled, pass his hand lightly on her head with affection and ask her to go back, she would immediately return.

Babuji, we never felt any animosity towards Rukmini. Those who did were all smitten by her. A number of householder disciples started visiting the ashram more frequently. Their eyes would constantly seek Rukmini. All this made the atmosphere of ashram a little tense.

Suddenly, one day, everyone in the *akhra* heard Raghunandan singing:

Oh Brahman, oh great knowledge, your name is Rukmini.
Oh earth, your name is Rukmini,
This Himalaya and Ganga, this bird and tree,
This sky and field, all are beautiful by the reflection of Rukmini's beauty,
Oh the great avadhut, you are also a woman at the core,
Your name is also Rukmini.
Now I'll start my journey in search of you.

My time has come,
I've heard the call.

Babuji, on hearing this song, Rukmini came out fearlessly and worshipped Raghunandan by offering water, flower and sandalwood paste at his feet. Everyone was stupefied. More conservative sanyasins of the *akhra* were angry and scandalized. The Mohanta said, we have to inform the members of our other ashrams—Nirbani, Niranjani, Atal, Ananda and others. We would take appropriate action after consulting all of them.

But it was no longer necessary. Raghu absconded that night. Just disappeared. We searched every inch of Hardwar, but no trace of him could be found.

Rukmini was distraught, but calm. Two months passed away in this tension. Then suddenly, Rukmini's husband visited the ashram along with a group of people, some of them armed. They had come to take Rukmini away. Their charge against the ashram authorities was that she had been detained there by force. It was a huge scandal. The reputation of the ashram was at stake.

We denied all accusation. Rukmini herself also not only refuted all the charges fiercely, she also refused to go with them. But finally they took her away by force.

Babuji, I would not lie to you. Rukmini's departure pained me. And why should it not? After all, Rukmini was the leela-consort of my beloved Raghu. In the path of sadhana, a consort was only a spiritual process. Love between a man and woman should not enter there. But in the case of Raghunandan, Rukmini had acted as a key to open the door between his heart and knowledge. It was she who had helped the flower blossom in the dry plant of his heart.'

Mahavir got up to go. I pleaded with him, 'Before leaving, please tell me what happened to Rukmini?'

He replied, 'I can't say what exactly happened to her. But within a year, we heard that she had become the glamourous Muniabai of Lucknow.'

I asked, 'How did that happen?'

He said, 'I won't know. What I heard was that her husband was a timid person. He could not save her. On the way, the very ruffians who had accompanied him, took her to a hidden place and gang-raped her for days together.

Finally, Rukmini escaped from the clutches of the goons. She did not go to the police or seek anybody's help. I don't know who helped her to the world of the courtesans in Lucknow. But soon, her reputation as a captivating beauty grew.

But suddenly, she left everything in the prime of her glory and re-emerged in the new avatar of Ramjidasi. I don't know what purpose it served. Has she been able to advance the cause of religion? She is now the talk of entire Uttar Pradesh. Even the sanyasins in the *akhras* discuss her. Today, you saw her with your own eyes. She is still the dazzling flame. I don't know what *pralay*, catastrophe, will happen again around her. As far as I hear, she is now always in an ecstasy of *naam*-kirtan, of singing the glory of God. People say, she met Raghunandan in Lucknow. After that, she has undertaken this journey. I don't exactly believe in this gossip. Moreover, there is another issue...'

Mahavir stopped. I implored him to go ahead. He continued, 'It may be a rumour. The person who was playing the sarod is believed to be totally devoted to her. He was an ordinary clerk in Lucknow. But his dexterity in sarod was highly appreciated. It is said that every evening, he volunteered to play sarod with Muniabai's dance. Now, he is her constant companion. He does not talk much. Not even with Ramjidasi. But the tune of his sarod speaks. Without the tune of his sarod, Ramjidasi's feet do not find the right step to dance, nor the right voice to sing.'

Mahavir smiled at this point and said, 'Babuji, many among the sanyasins know all this. Still you wanted to hear from me...'

'But what about Raghunandan?'

He again smiled an inscrutable smile and said, 'Raghunandan? The love-intoxicated mendicant? He destroyed my normal disciplined life. He gave me the mantra of love. He made me hear the songs of the bird, made me see the blue sky, made me understand the call of the heart; that became my nemesis. I could no longer remain a sanyasin. I left that life and became a mendicant seeker.'

Mahavir folded his palms on his forehead and took leave by saying, 'Namastey, Babuji,' then rapidly walked away towards the eastern side of the Kumbh-mela. The sand-bed path led to a slope beyond which Mahavir soon vanished out of sight. But the strain of the long story that he retold me remained afresh in my mind. The love story of Raghu and Rukmini was not the ordinary love story of the material world. I did not even comprehend the full import of the mystery, for I was an average domestic person trying to look at life through the glass of reason. But Raghu looked at the concept of love through the prism of spirituality. Love touched his heart in such a manner that Sanyasi Raghu became a *baul*—a mendicant, a seeker. And Rukmini? Who knew what mystery was hidden behind her crooked smile? Suddenly, the sarod-playing clerk gained stature in my eyes. Maybe, he had been able to discover that intriguing persona of Rukmini; otherwise, why her feet did not find rhythm of dance without the sound of his sarod?

I felt an urge to look at the man more closely. Perhaps it was too late, perhaps the programme was over. As I started back towards the ashram, I found a lot of people still roaming around. It was quite cold by then. Everyone was moving towards his or her respective tent. The moon had climbed almost up to the mid-sky.

Suddenly, I was jolted back to attention by the sound of the lashing of a whip. A tonga was entering the sand-bed. Its wheels were digging into the sand. The horse was finding it difficult to run. The passengers were looking around with sleepy eyes. Then the tonga-driver thrust the whip in his waist-band and jumped down to lift the wheel from beneath the sand. All this time, he was swearing at the wheels for their misdemeanour. Once his work was accomplished, he again started driving the tonga. A passenger from inside the tonga shouted in a sleepy voice, '*Kya, bimariwala ghora ley aya*? Have you brought a sick horse? I won't give you the full fare.'

What the tongawala replied in his rustic Hindi would mean, 'Yeah, the god of Kumbh-mela has settled on your shoulders only. And I am to return home empty-handed, *shala*.'

I smiled at this exchange and was about to turn back when someone came and stood in front of me. He bared his large teeth in the semblance of a smile and stared at me with his big round eyes. Before I could ask anything, he enquired in a hushed but excited tone, 'Have you got something?'

I was totally flummoxed. The man spoke in chaste Hindi. His whole body was covered in an expensive shawl. It was impossible to guess his age, but there was a conspiratorial look on his face. I was sure he had mistaken me to be someone else.

I asked, 'Are you speaking to me?'

He replied in an exuding voice, 'Who else, Maharaj?'

I queried, 'What did you ask?'

Again, he asked in a whisper, as if trying to pry a secret from me, 'Got something?'

This time I was a bit intrigued. I asked, 'I don't understand. What am I supposed to get, sir?'

The man nodded his head like a super-intelligent person and countered, 'Why are you hiding it, Maharaj? I've been watching you for quite some time. How can you dupe me? I know you won't share it with me. Nobody does. Just want to know if you've really got it?'

I felt irritated and said, 'What rubbish are you saying? What would I get and from whom?'

Totally unfazed, the man replied, 'Why, haven't you been talking to the sadhuji for the last two hours? And that too in a low tone. I've noticed everything. Maharaj, you are lucky. Not everyone gets such a break. But please tell me, *thoda bahut*—a little of it.'

I did not know whether to laugh or cry. How full of surprises was this congregation of lakhs of people! I had a different wave flowing through my mind. That got a jolt. I was going to see that sarod player once more. But this fellow started nagging in a totally different tune.

Still irritated, I asked, 'What do you think I might have got?'

The man laughed with his head bent on one side and said, 'My God, if I knew that, I would not be standing here. Brother, I've turned my hair grey by observing all this. You cannot hoodwink me.'

What a blackguard! I started walking. He also walked side by side. After a while, he asked, 'Have you seen the huge precious stone shop on the bank, just at the entrance of the mela?'

I said, 'No, I didn't.'

He laughed intriguingly with dancing eyebrows and said, 'Then you have missed a lot. That man is now a millionaire, you know. But once he used to beg on the streets of Lucknow. Then I noticed in one Kumbh-mela, he was tagging along constantly with a sadhu. After some time, I found that he had opened a small shop in a dark and narrow shed at the town. He started selling small stone icons of Shiva-linga, Mahadev, Vishnu and others. By the next Kumbh-mela, he became a full-fledged businessman, dealing in stone icons of various types. How did it all happen? Because of that companionship with the sadhu. I know all this, brother. You cannot dupe me.'

I was dumbfounded. This man was also a seeker, but seeker of what? Millions? At Kumbh-mela? On this sand-band? Just by running after a sadhu? Good God, I could not even imagine it.

This time I firmly said, 'I've not got anything. You are wasting your time.'

Obviously, he did not believe me. His appearance hardened. That ingratiating look was gone. The smile vanished. He scrutinized me with a pair of hard, sharp eyes. There was slight tremor in his body despite the expensive shawl cover. Was it anger or despair? I was not sure.

At that time, a huge commotion was seen, along with a clinking sound. Both of us turned to see the source of the sound. A tall and big sadhu was walking towards the east, stark naked. His great locks of matted hair were tied upwards. A number of garlands were dangling around his neck. He was carrying a long trident in his hand. Something tied around his trident was making the clinking sound, as his hands swayed in rhythm.

All the people had stopped in their track and were looking at him mesmerized. Some touched their foreheads with folded hands. Some picked up a pinch of sand from where his feet had touched it and put it on their heads.

Suddenly, an ecstatic sound came out from the throat of the man in front of me. His face lit up. All the despair of a few moments back was gone. He took off his shawl and tied it around his waist. Then giving me an utterly contemptuous look, he said, 'I've got it, I've got it.' With this declaration, he started following that naked sadhu with a feline grace, like a cat, as if a hunter was approaching his prey.

I could not laugh even at this ridiculous scene. Looking at the wet sand, I saw lakhs of footsteps. Lakhs of people were roaming about in this fair. They were carrying lakhs of desire, greed and other attractions of worldly life. All were rushing after the coveted goal. My erstwhile companion was also one such person. I did not know anything about his home, his family. He must have been running after the source of that million throughout his life. He must have whispered, 'Got it, got it' a number of times. All futile. At the end of the day, when the realization would dawn upon him about the futility of this mad rush, two drops of tears would surely trickle down his eyes. Would he remember me on that day? As someone who got everything in a Kumbh-mela, but deprived him of the knowledge? Strangely, my lips did not curl in a contemptuous smile. On the contrary, a deep pathos engulfed my heart at this futility and deprivation.

The cold was almost unbearable now. I walked back fast to the ashram. The noise had come down by then. The ashram courtyard was also almost deserted. I took shelter in the warmth of my makeshift bed.

When I got up in the morning, the tent was virtually empty. Snatches of conversation were coming from behind the tent. I put on my clothes and went out to wash my mouth. There was a long queue in front of the water tap. There was no point in standing in that queue. A welcome sunshine was wiping away the biting cold of the night. I moved away towards the bamboo fence to enjoy the sun alone.

The fair had already started coming alive. People's movement had begun. The bhajans and announcements on the microphone also. The tongawalas' shouting, the honking of the donkey carts, hooting of the lorries, horns of the private cars—the cacophony had already reached the tempo. A temporary path had been paved on the sand-bed. A kind of straw-like grass had been spread and solid earth placed on it. Maybe, it would ease the movement of the people to some extent.

A bunch of women were walking past the fence. Some were singing in a high-pitched voice, some were giggling. Their veils had been displaced from their heads in abandon. The cowherd was going with huge cows, shouting, 'Milk? Do you want hot milk?'

I had a toothbrush in my mouth. I would have loved to hear a hawker shouting—'Tea? Would you want tea?'—at this time.

Suddenly, I was jolted by a woman's eager voice, 'Babu, *meri* babu!' Almost immediately, a hand reached out through the gap in the fence and touched me. It was dirty, but fair. The nails were broken, but the fingers were long and slender. There were a few colourful glass bangles at the wrist. I looked at her face. Her hair was spread on her shoulder. The eyeballs were restless and sharp. A dirty copper ring was adorning her thin nose. A smile lurked in the corner of her mouth. The bright sunshine and the shade of the fence were playing on her face.

I asked, 'What do you want?'

She replied, 'Babu *meherbaan*. Please give me two paisas.'

Was she begging? Good God, what a way to beg! Smile on the lips, light in the eyes, hand touching my body. It was almost like a childish fanciful demand. Where was the pity of begging?

While I put my hands in the pocket in search of a coin, I noticed that she was wearing a light mill-produced sari with black border. It was worn in a fashionable style. Beneath the sari she had a bright red cheap blouse. She was tall and healthy looking. Maybe a little on the wilder side.

As I put a two-anna coin in her hand, I heard a hue and cry, 'Be on guard, all of you. That terrible woman has made another attempt to rob our camp. That bitch!' The girl laughed out mirthfully and vanished in a trice.

Even before I could realize what was happening, I found myself surrounded by the women army of the camp. The large woman named Khan-*pishi* was in the lead. She put herself squarely in front of me. Hearing the great noise, even Kotwalji came rushing forward.

Khan-*pishi* asked, 'You have given her money, haven't you?'

I was thoroughly scared, looking at Khan-*pishi*'s ferocious face. Others were also staring at me with suspicion. I mumbled out feebly, 'Yes, I have.'

'How much?'

'Two annas.'

'Two annas? So much?' Khan-*pishi* commented with enough venom. 'So you were bewitched by her face.'

I said, 'She begged. I felt like giving. Is it a crime?'

A young female voice reacted in a hushed tone, 'My God. How could you?'

It was Brajabala. Di'ma was also there. Everyone was astonished by my act of piety.

Still unable to comprehend the problem, I again asked sheepishly, 'What's wrong?'

Khan-*pishi* reacted sharply, 'What's wrong? Don't you know that she is a fallen woman, a thief, a bitch?'

So, this was the famous female thief. Not only goods-thief, but man-stealer also. I had totally forgotten about her. Now the realization dawned on me why I was uneasy about the contradiction in her demeanour and her act of begging.

I was never embarrassed so much in my life. Who knew that in the nectar of your generosity there could be so much poison? Everyone was looking at me with open contempt. I had nothing more to do apart from averting their eyes. Taking the brush out of my mouth, I thought of saying something and putting an end to this episode.

But that was not to be. The discussion among the ladies had taken a new turn. It was being debated who saw the bitch first. Of course, Khan-*pishi* with her huge bulk and shrillest voice won that honour.

She said, 'O my my, I was collecting water in my pitcher. Suddenly I saw her tugging at his hand and smiling coquetously. And he was telling her something in a melting tone.'

The more she narrated the encounter investing it with her own colour, the more the women looked at me with utter disgust. Fie! fie! As if it had been proved that my nature was to flirt with corrupt women. During the last two days, I was not particularly noticed by anybody. But this ordinary incident today had made me infamous. Especially among the Bengali circle. More so among the women.

There were ample whispering and a lot of derisive laughter. People started enquiring into my background: Where did I hail from? Who I had come with? Who I had been staying with? Even why had I come to the pilgrimage at this young age? And that too, alone?

Complicated issue. Suspicious looks. And yet, what had I done? Had just given some money to a beggar. I could not even recollect the face of the tricky woman. Only her sharp laughter was ringing in my ears.

In Balaram's laughter, there was an expression of boundless joy. Shyama's laughter was fraught with a suppressed agony. But the laugher of this girl? It was like the cooing of a sly bird in a vast expanse of land. The solitary wayfarer would be startled to hear it and look around.

Oh God, I could not look at Brajabala's eyes. Her young innocent eyes were as if telling me, 'Fie! fie! So, this is your real nature. Never call me Bouthan again.'

Kotwalji smiled a sweet, but crooked, smile. It had the hint of pseudo sympathy. He said, 'Dangerous woman, sir. Like a she-leopard. There are scores of them in this mela. If you lower your guard a bit, you are done for.'

Then lowering his voice, he said in a completely un-sanyasi-like tone, 'She chose her target well.' Saying so, he smiled meaningfully and left.

Totally devastated, I made for the tent. I did not dare to go to the water tap side anymore. But I could not move, for two large liquid eyes were staring at me from under the thick lense with what seemed like open admiration. An old woman stood on my way. Her face was fair, but full of wrinkles. Her hair was mostly grey. She was wearing a white sari, as the Bengali widows usually did.

She said, 'Wait, young man.'

Surprised, I asked, 'Do you want to tell me something?'

She did not reply to my question directly. After a few moment's pregnant silence, she said, 'You've done the right thing by giving the beggar money. If one cannot give here, what's the point of coming to a pilgrimage?'

I was quite surprised at this support from an unexpected quarter. The cloud that covered my mind cleared away and the sun again started shining in my heart. As I remained silent, the old woman again said, 'Tell me, who is more wretched in this world than the one who cannot give?'

I did not know what to say in reply. She kept looking at me for a few seconds. Then again she said, almost meditatively, 'One who gives also takes away. Everyone in this world comes to give and take. Mother gives to the son. Later, she takes from the son with open palm. You give to mother earth, then mother earth will give you back with full barn. The disciple takes from the guru. Later, when he becomes learned, he gives to his own followers. What other pleasure is there than giving?'

I felt embarrassed. I had given just two annas to a beggarwoman. And this old lady is talking about almost cosmic gift, from earth to the sky. From finite to infinite. My head automatically bowed down. I was a vagabond, roaming around with an empty jhola. My intention was to fill it with *amrita* (nectar) from others. How could I brag about my giving capacity?

But the old woman continued, 'I've liked you a lot, my son. I am the widow of a milkman. My son's name is Hriday. So, everyone calls me "Hriday's mother". Can I talk to you for a while? Come, sit here.'

I was feeling a little uneasy, because the Khan-*pishi* brigade were watching me. They must be thinking of this encounter as an undue fuss. Still, I did not feel like disappointing Hriday's mother. I sat down on the sand and waited for her to talk.

She also sat down and said, 'My son, there is no peace of mind at home. So, I come rushing out. But I see more restlessness in the outside world. Then I again run back home. For me, the inside and the outside have become the same. I don't know where I would find some peace.'

I asked, 'Why do you feel so restless?'

She replied, 'Everybody calls me Hriday's mother, but Hriday does not call me mother!'

'Why so?'

'For, I am not like a mother. They say, I am quarrelsome, jealous, termagent, gossip-monger and daughter-in-law hater.'

'Who says these things?'

'Neighbours and others. Now, even I say so. Otherwise, the same Hriday who would never eat without me serving him the food, now does not even look at me once. Selling milk, I sent him to school. Now, he works in an office at Calcutta, but would never send a single rupee for me. Why? Because I am no longer his mother.'

I could not respond to this story. I did not know the background. Who knew how much injustice, how much misunderstanding was there? Still, my heart felt heavy in empathy with Hriday's mother.

She opened her high-powered glasses and wiped her tears. Then said, with a hurt feeling, 'Let him not care for me. I manage by selling milk. And a few good men like you are there. Will you give me a few annas, son?'

I was taken aback. Was this another style of begging? My mind shrank like a snail. I watched her closely. The same eager face, the same expression of appreciation for me. There was no apparent change in her simple demeanour. Still, my cultured mind, which opened up its petals a few minutes back, started closing up.

Hiding my real feeling, I said, 'Sure, here you are!'

She caught hold of my hand that had gone inside the pocket and said, 'No hurry, son. You can give it later. Now, tell me what it is in your pocket. Is it the device with which you write?'

What would she need a pen for, I wondered and replied, 'Yes, fountain pen.'

She gave me an embarrassed smile and asked, 'Will you write a letter for me?'

I got curious and asked, 'Whom do you want to write the letter to?'

She again surprised me by saying, 'To Hriday. Whatever he does to me, I won't be at peace if I don't inform him that I am happy at the Kumbh-mela.'

I proceeded towards the tent with Hriday's mother on trail. Suddenly, I saw Brajabala. Her face and eyes expressed both anger and agony. The moment I entered the tent, she came with a pot of water for washing my face. As I stretched my hand to take it, she whispered in a scared voice, 'That stingy woman. I warn you, do not give her a single paisa.'

My mind filled up with mirth, sorrow and astonishment—all at the same time. It is Brajabala who turned out to be my real friend. She had told me about this miserly woman and that dangerous girl thief yesterday. There was sufficient advance warning. Only, I had forgotten all this.

Washing my hands and face, I fished out a white sheet of paper from my bag and sat down to write the letter.

Hriday's mother said, 'Address: Shri Hridayram Ghosh, etc. Also write the address of this ashram somewhere.'

Then she said, 'My son, Hriday...' and stopped to think. I guessed I would have to write a long one. I was yet to get a cup of hot tea in this cold winter morning. My mind was desperate to get rid of this woman as soon as possible.

Suddenly, she blurted out, 'My son, Hriday, I touch your feet. Please inform me how you all are—Nelo, Gopal, Parul, everyone. Your mother, the enemy.'

I said, '*Bya*s? Is that all? You said you wanted to inform him about yourself, didn't you?'

Hriday's mother replied, 'About myself? I have said it on the roads, in the temples and at the bank of Ganga. Even He who hears without being told has not heard me. What is the point of saying it again?'

My heart again ached for her. Let alone her God, if Hriday had heard her agonized prayer, her life would have filled with joy. Her home would have filled with the *amrita-kumbh* (pitcher of nectar). Life was full of such dramas of smile and tears. Some of them are strange and pathetic.

Handing over the letter to her, I looked for a coin. There was a two-anna bit, a four-anna bit and a rupee. I picked up the rupee and gave it to her.

Hriday's mother raised her eyes and exuded, 'A full one rupee, son? All right. I don't seek from one and all. You touched my heart. So, I didn't hesitate to ask you.'

Tucking the coin in the border of her sari, she left. I also came out of the tent. Brajabala was standing with her eyes fixed at the sky. Her head was covered with the end of her sari. She cast a fiery glance at the receding figure of Hriday's mother. Obviously, she was furious that I had given her money. Not surprising, as she was my real friend.

Brajabala said, 'Di'ma has asked you to take your meal before leaving.'

'Now?'

'Yes, we'll go out today.'

She was really cross. I said, 'I'll eat after coming back.'

'We shall leave soon. If you are late, your food will be kept covered in the tent.'

I smiled and said, 'That's all right.'

Suddenly, Hriday's mother shouted from the gate, 'Daughter-in-law, o daughter-in-law!'

At once, Braja came running to me and said, 'That's her.'

I could not connect and asked, 'What are you talking about?'

By that time, Braja's anger had totally vanished. She was still so young that her emotions fluctuated quickly. Her eyes widened, as she told me, 'That poor woman I told you about. One whose husband has relinquished household and become a sadhu. One who has come here with her brother-in-law in search of the lost husband. Don't you remember?'

I remembered. The woman was tall and fair. Fashionably dressed. She was wearing a blue sari and a matching light pink lady's coat. The morning sunlight shone on the vermillion on her forehead and the parting of her hair. She was accompanied by a rather hefty young man. He was wearing a modern alistar and a pair of thick-framed spectacles. He was speaking to the lady with a smile in his face. They stopped on hearing the call of Hriday's mother. Once she reached them, all three were lost in the forest of crowd.

Braja commented, 'The two look quite matching, isn't it?'

That was true. Such observations defied age. Otherwise, how did it dawn on young Braja? Why did she make this comment in the first place, I wondered.

I came out for a round in the fair. Today, it looked more gorgeous. The crowd movement was also more than yesterday. Moving on the northern side, I suddenly saw a signboard on a tent—North Western Restaurant. Within brackets, it announced 'Vegetarian'. The front of the tent was decorated with multi-coloured flowers and garlands—made of paper. A liveried attendant was standing outside. I peeped in to find that it was empty. The inside was not well-lit; it was rather a little darkish. Chair and table were placed on the sand. At some places, there were wooden platforms beneath the chair and table.

I was thirsty for tea. A boy approached me with a printed menu. The urban paradise at the fair ground, I thought. Without looking at the menu, I ordered tea and toast.

Next moment, I noticed a man sitting at the corner chair. On the table in front of him there were pen, paper, inkpot and a flower vase. The gentleman was looking at me. Once our eyes met, he raised his hands by way of greeting.

I guessed he must be the proprietor of the restaurant. I also returned his greeting by touching my forehead. Immediately, the gentleman got up and walked down to me.

He asked in English, 'Have you ordered?'

I replied, 'Yes.'

Those who are experts in striking up a conversation with an unknown person do not need any introduction. Moreover, those who are eager to talk to a stranger would not mind asking a sudden personal question. The gentleman smiled and said, 'You must have come from Bengal.'

I parried, 'How did you know?'

This time he answered in clear Bengali, 'The Hindi you were using with the boy was a perfect giveaway. This is the typical Bengali Hindi.'

I had to concede the point. Then I asked, 'You are also a Bengali?'

The gentleman sat down on the chair opposite to me and spread out his feet. Then he asked in English with a quiz-master like smile, 'Take a guess.'

Now I felt a little unsure. If language was a marker, he should be a Bengali. But his features belied it. He was six feet tall, with broad forehead and back-brushed curling black hair. His fair complexion was slightly sun-tanned. The most noticeable aspects in his appearance were a few deep creases on his forehead and cheeks. His smile was amiable, but his face could turn terrible if he got angry. He wore European clothes, but all very shabby. Dirty shirt, greasy tie and a worn out coat. Considering all, it was difficult to think of him as a Bengali.

He was still looking at me with a challenge showing in the smile of his lips. I was about to say, 'You are a non-Bengali.' Then I looked at his eyes. It seemed that the smile in his lips had not touched his eyes. Through those serious pair of eyes peeped a different person. A vagabond wayfarer, an adventurer.

I blurted out, 'You must be a Bengali.'

The gentleman erupted in jubilant emotion and said, 'Right, my brother. Give me your hands. The non-Bengalis easily identify me as a Bengali. But Bengalis often decide that I am a non-Bengali.'

Without waiting for my response, he took my palms in his huge paws and shook them. The he shouted, 'How Ramaiya?'

In response, there was a strange sound from within the tent. The gentleman spoke something in a rapid unintelligible tongue. The reply also came from inside in the same alien language.

I was looking at him with astonishment. What language was the man speaking?

He guessed my bewilderment and said in suppressed excitement, 'Do you know which language I spoke?'

'No.'

'It's Telugu. I was asking why your tea was taking so long.'

Almost on cue, the tea arrived in a tray. All components were served separately. Even the butter for the toast. I told myself that I was no longer in the Kumbh-mela, but in a civilized cultured world.

Removing the cover of the teapot, I found that there were at least three cups of tea. I asked the boy to give me another empty cup and requested the gentleman to join me. After initial hesitation, he agreed.

The gentleman kept on blabbering, as I was having the toast and he was pouring the tea, '*Moshai*, never be fastidious about food. This is a bad habit. I was also quite choosy earlier. Once something interesting happened. I was in Karachi. That is before the Partition. The city was spick and span. Not a single beggar was seen on the main roads. The law was very strict in that regard. But if you go inside the lanes, you will find dirt and soot and scum. People fight at the drop of a hat. I had a friend—an Abyssinian coolie leader named Yakub. Once he invited me to his house. You won't believe what I saw. Handmade rotis, at least ten days old. Worms were quite visible in them. And what came as mutton was simply obnoxious; it must have been the entrails of a ship. As I was hesitating, he said with sarcasm, "I've heard that the Bengalis like to eat the stem of a banana tree. Maybe, this roti-meat will not suit you." I was cut to the quick at this jibe at the Bengalis and ate everything with apparent relish. It is another story that after coming out of his house, I stuck my finger in the throat and retched out the whole thing.'

'Then I invited him home as a return favour and offered him two days old soaked rice and jaggery. This was my tit for tat. But, my friend, you won't believe that the fellow ate it to his heart's content, so much so that my stock exhausted when he was asking for more. I was greatly embarrassed.

While leaving he commented, '*Bohut barhiya cheeze khilaye dost*, you have fed me a wonderful dish, my friend.' I shrank in shame. From that day onwards, I realized that when you venture out, you have to adapt to the local custom and local food. There is no point in clinging to your own Bengali habits everywhere.'

Suddenly, he changed the topic and asked, 'What's your name, brother?'

I told him.

'Good name. Do you have any relative in Allahabad?'

'No.'

'Where have you put up then?'

I told him the name of the ashram. That brought a suppressed smile in his mouth. He now asked in a more intimate tone, 'Well, brother, why so much apathy towards worldly interest in this young age?'

I replied, 'No apathy at all. There was an inner call. So, I hit the road. The desire is to roam about and see it all.'

While sipping his tea, he asked, 'Where will you roam about? What do you want to see?'

He said this with such detachment as if there was nowhere to go and nothing to see.

I looked at him. His gaze was fixed at the horizon. As if he was trying to see something afar. There was a play of light and shade in his eyes. Suddenly, he said again,

'Look, I'm really an ordinary person. May blurt out some nonsense. Once I read the Bengali translation of a Japanese poem. It read like this:

What do I do, where do I go?
Where is there peace for me?
Thought I'll cool my heart
By living in the forest;
There I heard the tremulous cry of a doe at midnight.

He fell silent. I could detect a deep suppressed agony in his voice. The way in which he suddenly embraced total silence was as if inducing the other person also to remain mute. I had abandoned my groove and had taken to the road with an intense desire to see and discover. My eyes were eager to see, my mind was like a free bird and my ears were alert to hear. There was a call of the unknown and the unseen in my heart. But this gentleman was as if trying to stifle all my curiosity with his closed fist. I did not know what to say.

The noise outside was increasing. I could hear loud conversation and occasional shouting outside the tent. Thousands of people were moving about on the sunlit sand-bed. So many people—men, women, young and old as well as children had converged from the whole country. Like me. I did not know who had given them the clarion call, what tune had played in their heart. As for myself, I did not even know what restlessness was there rooted deep in my soul.

I remembered a song that I had heard long ago. I did not know whether it was written in Chinese or Japanese. But it communicated in the language of the heart. I was sitting in front of the grocery shop of my locality and a street singer was singing:

I anchore my boat in many moorings
But do not get to see you,
When I ask someone at home
Pat comes the reply, 'Who are you talking about?'
I ask everyone, I ask around in the forest,
Alas! The forest also cries and tells me,
'Couldn't get to see him.'

The same suppressed agony. But still should you stay idle without any attempt to seek? I remembered Balaram. My wanderer eyes had also seen Shyama, whose laughter was perhaps fraught with the cry of that midnight doe. As I was about to say something, he said, 'Whenever you go, this will go with you.'

He pointed his finger at his own heart. Then immediately added,

'Does it ever fill up? It doesn't. And that's why all this longing to see and feel.'

He smiled. His huge copper-complexioned rough and rugged face looked piteous when he smiled.

Again he said, 'And yet we are restless, for we want to fill it up. We do not know that the pot has a hole. The more we fill it up, the more it becomes empty. Do you know that there is a lovely song in Hindi. It says, 'You wench, you have brought water from the Yamuna in your *gagri*, your pitcher. But what magic! All your water spills over and falls down. Then you again run to the Yamuna. I say, what is this filling and emptying game you are playing? Is the dark water of

Yamuna so playful like a naughty child that it does not want to sit still in your *gagri* (pitcher)?'

He laughed out. Biting cold wind entered the tent rustling the screens. The tip of his sticky tie moved in the wind like the raised hood of a snake.

Remaining silent for a moment, he again said, 'That which did not fill up in life—will it be full at death?'

The gentleman had come uninvited to strike up a conversation with me. But his nature enticed me to such an extent that I could not take leave of my own volition. His faraway lost look, his weather-beaten face and his helpless smile had simultaneously created a pain and a curiosity in my mind.

I asked, 'Where is your home?'

This time, he really roared in laughter. Then said, 'So, our adda over tea is gathering momentum, right? You are asking personal questions. But brother, I've no homeland. Although I was born in a village in West Bengal, I left home at the age of eighteen. Since then, I have been a vagabond, a wayfarer.'

I pushed further, 'Where are your folks—father, mother, other relatives?'

'Brother, I don't remember to have seen my father. Lost my mother also quite early. An aunt brought me up till the age of eighteen. She had some landed property; she also owned a big house, cows and other livestock. When she died, a number of nephews and nieces came to claim their share of all this. Strangely, instead of being peeved, I felt relieved.

That was my first realization that I did not want to remain attached to anything.'

His face and eyes turned dreamy at this point. He went on telling me, 'When I was young, my mother would point her finger at the bamboo grove and say, "Beware! Never go to that side." But I would keep staring at the bamboo grove throughout the day. Every Bengali living in a village knows how the rustling of the wind at the bamboo grove sounds like a beckoning call—"Come, come hither!" That sound still lingers in my ear. Through the openings of the bamboo grove, I would see the field stretched far and wide. Believe me, somebody called me from that field also. I could not study in school. So, once my wings grew, I fled home. That day was a very special day for me. I was brimming with joy. Now I realize what a terrible day it was!'

Perplexed, I asked, 'Why?'

His face contorted into a hundred creases. There was obvious expression of deep pain.

He said, 'You want to know why? I don't know which evil spirit hypnotized me into deserting my home and hearth. Now, there is no path to move forward, no way to go back; I am circling around in a labyrinth. I've heard that many people undertake travels to write travelogues. I hate those books. They do not know how dreadful is the actual addiction of a globetrotting life.'

He fell silent. I felt as though I was hearing the remorse of a drunkard. Once he had drunk wine to his heart's content. Now the poisonous reaction had set in. But as such, a wayfarer had his share of joy also. I never knew that the way could take revenge like this.

Suddenly I asked, 'You did not tell me your name.'

He laughed out loudly and replied, 'I've a terrible name. That's also a joke on my vagabond life. Well, you will have to order another round of tea if you want to know it.'

I said, 'Most certainly.' But before I could call the boy, he ordered tea in his chaste Telugu.

I asked, 'Haven't you been to Bengal after that?'

'Of course. Many times. But I've visited my village only once. It was just after the War. I roamed around the village the whole day. No one recognized me. The grocer of the village, Haren Mudi, was sitting outside his shop. He had become old, his skin had become loose. He asked me in Hindi, '*Kya mangta, saab* (What do you want, sahib)?' I said, '*Pouwa bhor chira deo, aur do paise ki gur* (Give me a quarter of flattened rice and jaggery worth two paise).' He enjoyed great pleasure in treating the sahib with flattened rice and jaggery.'

We had finished drinking our tea. It was time to take leave. He said, 'Please do come again. There is none here with me; I can talk frankly.'

I got up and said, 'The name?'

'Oh, you've not forgotten? Well, my name is Ramanimohan Mukhopadhyay.' Saying so, he started laughing convulsively. Finally, he said, 'How can I be the charmer (*mohan*) of ladies (*ramani*)? Ha ha ha.'

As I started walking, I wondered how this extremely handsome, tall man could end up being a vagabond. There was a tired, helpless persona inside his apparent façade of joviality.

After a few steps, I turned back. He was still standing in front of the tent. I said loudly, 'Can I tell you something?'

'Yes, sure.'

'You asked me why I had come to Kumbh-mela. I would not have met you, had I not come.'

He burst into a guffaw and shouted back, 'Then your pilgrimage is futile this time. Your *kumbh* (pitcher) will remain empty, brother. Ha ha ha….'

His laughter floated to me in the northern wind. I did not know whether my empty pitcher would be filled, but I could definitely say that my heart was filled to the brim by discovering this extraordinary person. In fact, what mattered ultimately was the humanity. My appetite for seeing mankind more closely, to share their feelings further increased after this encounter. The variety was endless, the beauty was boundless.

I started walking towards the east. There were people all around. All dressed in various colours. There was great noise; people were busily running around. They were pushing forth straight forward, backward, to their right, to their left. I felt a great surge of joy in my mind. A thousand tunes played there by the jingling of one string. I felt as if I was not walking alone. Lakhs of people were walking with me. I was one of them. They were as if keeping step with me, maintaining rhythm with my movement. As if everyone had received a call to the east.

The sand-band in front had now become undulating. The number of tents was less on this side. The sand was also drier and whiter. The huge number of people walking on it were looking like a forest on the move. Then there were tongas carrying men and women. Occasional private cars were plying, raising a lot of dust to the disgust of the surrounding crowd. From above the village of Kushi, a drove of camels was coming down carrying dry logs on their back. Their swaying movements from a distance were looking like the waves of an ocean. A flock of donkeys was also coming. On their back, there were vegetables and fruits. It was a strange congregation of man, animal and nature.

Amidst laughter and conversation all around, the blind Surdas was walking with his stick extended to navigate. There was song in his throat. I did not understand its language, but I could gauge that it was full of liberation and joy. It seemed he did not feel cold as intensely as we did. His body was bare, a dirty worn out stole was tied around his waist. His dry unkempt hair was flowing in the wind. At times, he would stop and ask, 'Hello dear, do you hear? Am I going in the right direction?' It sounded like a symbolic question, as he did not care to listen to any reply. He would laugh loudly and then again break into a song.

***

Suddenly, a storm surged in the sand-bed. Where did it materialize from? Which way was the tornedo going?

Nobody knew. We, a huge bunch of people, were abruptly drawn into the vortex of the storm. Our path was blocked, we were helpless. Oh the pious one, give, give! Oh the kind one, give, give! Oh, the king and the queen, give, give!

The storm was raised by a group of women beggars. They were seeking money, but all with smiling faces. They were all clad almost in the same kind of clothes. The saris were dirty and worn out, dry unkempt hair, and unclean faces. But strangely, there were vermillion marks on their foreheads. Even if we, the pilgrims, felt pestered and stumped, still we were not angry. There was a jocund atmosphere. I put my hand in the pocket of my coat to fish out some coins. Suddenly, my eyes fell upon the girl with the red blouse and peacock-bordered sari. The one who 'bewitched' me in the morning, according to Khan-*pishi*. There she was camouflaged among the beggars, but she looked different. Maybe it was my polluted eyesight. Maybe it was my corrupt mind. But I gave her money for a second time that day. She held my eyes with a mesmerizing stare. There was that sharp, crooked smile on her lips. Her smile was the smile of victory. Her look was the look of deception. The loosened border of her sari had fallen off her shoulder, but she did not seem to care.

I averted my eyes. My civilized mind took over. But I wondered how to describe the attraction or the appeal of this girl. She was as if like a curved sword of steel, dazzling in the reflection of the sun. I could not gauge the nature of this nomadic beggar. While she was openly begging, she was not at all solicitous. As if, she was just demanding a favour from you. There was no attempt in her face, look and entire body language to evoke even a drop of pity.

So far as the other female beggars who stormed the fair, one always noticed a pattern. They were everywhere—in cities, markets and fairs. I have seen them moving in bunches on weekends in the suburbs of Calcutta. Despite their torn clothes, soiled faces and unkempt hair, they had a rhythm in their movement. And my disobedient eyes never failed to notice that although they were poor and ill-fed, their bodies were fully endowed with youthful beauty. We earn a lot of piety in our pilgrimages. We bow before idols in different temples for divine blessings. These beggars follow us only for a couple of coins. In doing so, they also willy-nilly cover a lot of pilgrimages. Does not a little of God's pity rain down upon their heads at all?

I was moving along the flood of bustling humanity while musing on these philosophical thoughts. Suddenly, someone asked from very near, 'Is it the right path?' It was Surdas, the blind singer. I did not know if he kept asking this question just for the heck of it. Still I replied, 'Yes, it is the right path.'

'Really?' He laughed out heartily. It sounded like the expression of a simple, naive mind. And yet, there was a trace of wonder in his voice. He again laughed and asked,

'Babuji, *aap ka raasta thik hai*?—Are you going in the right direction?'

Having said so, he looked at the sky with open mouth. The two white pupils of his eyes shone like silver under the sun, as if he was expecting a reply from the sky. I was slightly taken aback. What sort of question was this? I was a person with full eyesight. I gave a blind man direction for his way forward. How could he ask me a counter-question about my direction? Was he trying to make any metaphysical statement? Before I could say anything, he again laughed and elaborated, '*Koi nahi bata sakta kidhar gayi sadak, kahan gaya raasta! Hai na,* Babuji? No one can tell you where the road leads to? Isn't it, Babuji?' Even in that great din and bustle, his voice was calm and quiet.

I now realized that he had been repeatedly asking this question to himself. Many people had responded to his query, and he had only laughed within himself.

Someone called out, 'Hello, Surdas, why have you stopped singing?' Perhaps Surdas was rehearsing a song silently. He immediately broke into a song full-throatedly.

In front of me, the path rose over the highland of Kushi. A staircase with many steps needed to be climbed. Then the path took a bend behind a banyan tree. Beyond that a fort surrounded by walls was visible against the sky. Somewhere in the middle of the parapet, there was a cave. Another staircase from the cave had come down on the sand-band. Hundreds of people were climbing down that zigzag staircase. From a distance they looked like an army of ants.

I was told that it was the well of Samudragupta. But where was the well? It looked like a well-protected fort, standing tall with military gravity.

Observing the two staircases, I noticed that the southern one was for climbing up and the northern one was for climbing down. On the way up, there were a number of ancient banyan trees. This was providing shade on the stairs. Whichever way I looked, there were any number of such clumps of hundred-year-old banyan trees. From the earth to the sky. This had given the whole Kumbh location a touch of ancientness.

Blind Surdas had been tagging along with me. He asked from behind, 'Babuji, isn't there the staircase to climb upon the mound?'

Mound? Not the well of Samudragupta?

I replied, 'Yes, there's the staircase. But you won't be able to climb it, Surdas.'

He smiled, '*Nahi sakenge*? Won't be able to?' Asking this question, he raised his head towards the sky. Then he virtually stumped me by declaring, 'Babuji, this is not my first time. I've climbed it a number of times.'

We see so many blind people on our paths. Normally, we don't even look at them. Talking to them was out of the question. If anyone asks anything, we give a casual reply. At best, we demonstrate occasional kindness by giving the blind beggar a paise or two. That's about it.

But today, in this Kumbh-mela, I had to pause and look at the blind beggar closely. He is blind, but all his actions were like a person with sight. Behind his unselfconscious laughter, there was hidden a conscious active soul. His face betrayed an expression of fun and mystery. I was observing him; but for his words it would seem as if he was seeing me more.

With his characteristic smile, he again said, 'Babuji, everyone says it is difficult to climb, but easier to descend. But

I am blind since birth. For me, climbing is easy, descending is difficult.'

He laughed again. The way he laughed with his mouth open, one could see even the movement of his uvula.

Intrigued by his contrary opinion, I said, 'But Surdas, climbing is usually tougher, not climbing down.'

He said, 'Perhaps true. Perhaps, this is the experience of people like you with eyesight. But let me cover your eyes. You will see that you stumble when climbing down. Just think about it with your eyes closed.'

I was an educated urban gentleman. How could I agree to this strange argument? Moreover, it was not possible to visualize things with your eyes shut.

Surdas laughed like a drunken person and said, 'Thinking like that is pretty tough, isn't it, Babuji?'

He did not wait for my reply, but started singing in an undertone. I did not quite get the language, but could guess that he was cautioning a 'sajani' (she-friend) about something. Then he explained,

'After climbing at the top, whatever you get in your hand, keep it steady while climbing down, otherwise it will slip and fall. Looking for it won't be worthwhile. For, you are blind, mind you.'

I was startled. It seemed the caution was not just for the physically blind, but for all of us who were prone to be mentally blind.

Blind Surdas held forth, 'The great sages move against the current in the path of their sadhana. Why? Because they sail through the ocean of sin towards the upstream of piety. But, Babuji, who dares to move with the tide and climb down the sea. Everyone is scared of that path. For, it is strewn with sin and death. So, climb up carefully, but climb down even more carefully. If you think it is easy to descend, friend, you will slip and go astray. And the blind world will then laugh at you:

> *Sahaj samajke mat chaliho sajani,*
> *Raasta bahut terha hai*
> (Do not consider descent easy, friend;
> The road is very slippery)

I felt as if a curtain was removed from my eyes. It is absolutely true that all fall happens during descent. One does not fall when going up. Of course, it is so, because all worldly attractions are below. In our desire to reach them fast we miss our steps and fall. I could not see this truth with my eyes. I had to learn if from a blind man. I kept looking at him with beauty-blurred eyes, for I was seeing a seeker of truth.

I finally asked him, 'You always ask about the right path. Path leading to what, Surdas? God?'

He folded his hands and bowed before me, as if he was begging forgiveness. Then he said, 'Babuji, I don't know anything about God. The world is dark for me. I keep searching for light. Babuji, you only know what you are searching for. And path? There are a thousand paths. It is your mind that will decide which path you want to follow.'

Suddenly, he changed the direction of the conversation and asked quite matter-of-factly. 'Babuji, is there a shop of dry logs around?'

I looked around and found that there was really a shop of fuelwood nearby. Two youngsters, a boy and a girl were laughing with their backs on the heap of wood. Perhaps, they were enjoying the sun.

I said, 'Yes, there is. How do you know?'

'The wind carries the smell of the wood. Please guide me a little. I will sit there.'

'You are not going to climb?'

'No.'

I took his hand and led him towards the mound of fuelwood. As we did so, I asked, 'Why have you come here, Surdas? It's a lot of trouble for you.'

He laughed and said, 'Babuji, my home is dark, outside also is dark. Trouble is everywhere. Then where is joy?'

He felt the way with his stick and unerringly reached the shop and sat down. Then he turned his face towards me and smiled a sort of goodbye smile.

I walked towards the stairs for climbing upon the mound. On climbing a step or two, I realized that I should have given him a little money. I looked back and found that by now, he had hit it off with the two children. They were sitting on either side of him with their hands on his shoulders. Surdas was as if the manifestation of simple joy in life. The children could easily be his playmates. Perhaps, this was how he sought his light.

I climbed up the stairs. On top, there was a neat and clean tableland. There were a few small cabins on the left with their tops shaped like domes as in temples. Each of these cabins contained either a stone idol or at least just pebbles, smeared with vermillion. Most of the idols were broken; some had lost their hands, some legs and some faces. I realized that year after year these stone gods and goddesses lay asleep in these cells, perhaps hungry and thirsty too. Now that the season had come, they had been washed and cleaned. A panda sporting a tuft was seated in front of each cabin and extolling the greatness of the god or goddess concerned. It was followed by loud and shameless solicitations for donation. The ringing sound of the pilgrims' coins could be heard everywhere.

From the sand-bed, I climbed further up to a peaceful shadowy village—Kushi. It is also called Pratisthanpur. It was the domain of the Vatsa Kings. But where was Samudragupta's well here?

On my left, there was a house surrounded by a boundary wall. It looked like a common householder's dwelling. On the same side, there was also a quarry. From deep down the quarry, an ancient tree with thousand veins had come up straight. It had a luxuriant growth of leaves. Who had blessed it with so much greenery in this deserted place? For whom were all these blessings? Was it the well?

I peeped in. There were shadows of people in the quarry. I heard noises and conversations. As I watched closely, I saw a narrow path going down the quarry and a long row of people were walking through that path. That stream of people ended in a sort of a tunnel. Was it the well, then? But how to land in that path?

I looked up towards the south of the gorge. People were climbing on that path also. Perhaps, this has turned downwards somewhere beyond the bend. I joined the current of people on that path. It was so narrow that one had to move behind another. Hundreds like this, then thousands, then lakhs. The path was not new, but my journey surely was.

By the side of the path, sadhus were seated in bunches. Some puffing on their ganja chillums, but their vigilant eyes were observing every pilgrim. They were also on the lookout for donations.

Suddenly, I was forced to halt. There was a huge crowd ahead. Everyone was telling everyone, '*Jaane do, babua* (Let me go, dear).' They wanted to do darshan. I did not know which god was residing up above the hillock. The pilgrimage looked sad and indifferent. But there was 'Byom! Byom!' sound all around. Perhaps, it was the abode of Lord Mahadeva.

I was debating in my mind whether to go farther or give up when someone held me in a tight embrace from behind. I turned around to find an old Marwari woman sporting a colourful chunni. Her eyesight was quite dazed and her head was trembling like that of an old hen. On her dry grey hair, there was a gold tiara. A heavy gold necklace was around her neck like a shackle. Because of exhaustion, her tongue had come out. Her whole body was covered with dust like abir, coloured powder used during the Holi festival. She was perhaps not aware that I was a human being. She grasped me like a pole, just to keep her balance. But the problem was that because of her heavy weight, I was about to lose my balance.

After a few moments, the old woman looked up at me and smiled a toothless smile. It is difficult for me to describe how divine that smile was. Then she touched my head with her hand and again got lost in the crowd.

I decided to give up the darshan and moved away from the crowd towards the east. This side was more serene and beautiful. But not many people frequented it. All the crowding was at the doors of the temples, before their favourite deities. Through the gaps among the trees, one could see the chickpea field at a distance. On the northern plane, there were a few local villages. In the eyes of a Bengali, these villages might look a little ugly. As if they were not villages, but slums. The mud-huts did not have either awning or the walls of aquatic grass. There is a Hindi saying:

Chhaja baja kesh
Tino milke Bangladesh

Which means that the three distinct features of Bengal are the awning of its houses, the drum beats of its festivals and the hairstyles of its women.

While observing the village, I suddenly came across a drumstick tree. This tree was typical of Bengal. It brought me both joy and sorrow. Joy for obvious reasons. And the tinge of sorrow was due to the realization that I was away from home for many many days. There was a further surprise. The branches of the tree were trembling under the weight of fruits and flowers. The white fragrant flowers of the drumstick tree were falling underneath with dripping sound. And a red-sari-clad girl was eagerly collecting those flowers in the stretch of her drape-end, on her lap. As I watched her, she suddenly raised her head. A stunningly dark woman. Her head was uncovered. Long unkempt hair had cascaded down below her waist. There were absolutely no ornaments on her body. Only a rosary of rudraksh was strewn around her neck. But a vermillion mark was indistinctly visible at the parting of her hair. She was stockily built. The most striking features of her face were a pair of large liquid eyes, like those of the deities on images or in paintings. She stared at me openly without any hesitation. It was difficult to decipher that gaze: was there surprise and curiosity? Or anger and suspicion?

Who was this forest-dweller Kapalkundala that I had come across? There was no mysterious smile on her lips, nor any invitation in her eyebrows. Would this forest now come alive with her question, 'Have you lost your way, O wayfarer?'

But the drowsy forest did not wake up from its dream by any such voice. This hillock of Uttarpradesh did not create another narrative of the Kapalkundala of Kumbh-mela. A *kapalik* entered the scenario prematurely.

'Namaste, Babuji. Where are you coming from?'

From his trademark roundly pronounced Hindi, I could easily guess that he was a Bengali. Clad in red dhoti and a red stole, he had an unshaven thorny beard and a moustache. His eyes were red and half-closed, and his weight was around one *maund*. His hair was matted and a bunch of rudraksh rosaries were hanging like a burden from his neck.

I replied in Bengali.

Immediately, he enthused, 'Oh, I see. You belong to my land, Bengal.'

That was true. I was the modern Nabakumar, dressed in coat-pant. Perhaps the *kapaliks* were scared of these unknown elements, for he bowed down in all humility and said, 'Sir, my name is Adbhootananda Bhairav. People call me Bhootananda, some even Bhootbaba. I am a tantrik worshipper of Mother Goddess Kali. Originally, I belonged to Jessore. During the partition, our home fell in East Pakistan. To safeguard my religion, I crossed over to this side and set up an ashram in Barasat of the 24 Parganas. The woman here is my Bhairavi. I had a long cherished the desire to come to Prayag at a pilgrimage. So, here I am. Where do you hail from, sir?'

Well, here was a tantrik Kali worshipper, but his humility was like the vaishnavas. His Bhairavi was rather indifferent to this conversation. She was still busy picking up flowers.

I vaguely replied, 'I stay near Calcutta.'

He folded his palms and requested, 'Please come, Sir. Step into my ashram for a while.'

Though I could not see even the hint of an ashram anywhere, I followed Bhootananda. A little away on the east side there was a hut made of aquatic grass. The front was well dusted and clean. Decayed dry leaves had been collected in a huge pile at one corner of the courtyard. Over the roof of the hut, a red cloth was fluttering, perhaps the symbol of his sect. This was Bhootananda's ashram. Within the hut, there was a discoloured tin suitcase and a couple of aluminium boxes. A bed was made by spreading a blanket over a spread of hey.

Bhootananda requested me to sit down on the tattered blanket, 'Please take your seat, Sir. Let me talk to you about dharma with an open heart. This part is frequented by bears at night. At daytime some people come only to defecate. Mostly Punjabis and Marwaris. Even fair complexioned, well clad women also do it here. They don't care even if I make a discreet coughing sound. And yet, I have to be here for my sadhana. Now that you have blessed me with the dust of your feet—'

I realized that Bhootnath was expecting some religious discourse from me. But I was totally innocent of such knowledge.

Meanwhile, the Bhairavi sat down on the floor, a little distance away. She spread her feet in front of her and put down a bunch of drumsticks flowers from her lap on an aluminium pot. Then she gave me a fiery look with her large eyes and turned that look on the Bhairav. Her nostrils flared a little. I could sense a storm coming from her expression.

But the Bhairav was oblivious to all this. He seemed to be settling down for a long session of holy conversation. With half-closed eyes, he suddenly asked, 'Dadababu, tell me who owns the world?'

My God, such a seminal question! I did not know that such a philosophical issue was waiting for me in this isolated place on the Kushi hillock. After posing the question, Bhootananda indulged in a suppressed smile along with a mild shaking of the head. As if he was smuggly challenging my knowledge.

I did not know if my reply would satisfy him. Still I sincerely said, 'It would seem that humankind owns the world.'

Bhootananda was rather happy at my response. He opened the eyes for a moment, then closed them again and shot again, 'Good, you have answered half of it. But which section of humankind are you referring to?'

I failed to understand and asked naively, 'I don't get your point.'

Without opening his eyes, he promptly asked, 'Didn't you understand? The world belongs to man or woman, right sir?'

I have never learnt to differentiate humanity on the issue of gender. But the way in which Bhootananda was looking at me expectantly, I understood that this was the crux of his questioning. If I said, it belonged to both, he might not be happy. So I gave a diplomatic reply, 'Oh, I haven't thought about it.'

From his indulgent smile and shaking of head, I realized that he had expected this ignorance from me. Then he plucked up a handful of earth and asked, 'What is it called, sir?'

I was flabbergasted. Was he going to show some magic or what. I tentatively replied, '*Mati*, earth.'

'Yes, you are right, "mati" or "maa-ti" (the Mother). Which means what?'

At this point, he suddenly turned towards the Bhairavi and said, 'Lend me your ear too, Chandike.'

I guessed 'Chandike' meant 'Bhairavi', but could not guess why she should closely listen to our conversation. However, Bhairavi's reaction was spectacular. Her eyes flashed for a moment. It seemed lightning passed through her body. Her lips curled in a wry smile. She turned around on the other side, showing her back to us. Was this her way of listening attentively?

Bhootananda did not care to look towards her. His eyebrows danced when he pontificated, 'So, this earth is our mother, sir. It follows that the owner of the world is womankind, right, Dadababu?'

I tamely acquiesced, 'Perhaps, it is so.'

This time, Bhootananda rolled his huge head and said, 'But this mother also must have a mother, right?'

I shook my head in agreement. A mother would also have a mother—this sounded quite logical.

Now Bhootananda had reached the climax. With eyes opened wide, he fixed me in a gaze and asked, 'So, who is that mother?'

I had no clue. Bhootananda seemed to be rather pleased at my ignorance. Lowering his voice, he gravely said, 'Her name is Jagatmata Jagattarini, Shaktirupini, Maa Kali

(Mother Goddess Kali, the presiding deity of the world and embodiment of all power).'

Having declared it, he came closer to me and whispered, 'But I can tell you for certain. Maa Kali is not there in Prayag!'

I was quite surprised, for I was not aware of such a secret truth. I could only say, 'Is it so?'

'That's what I am telling you, sir. Go and take a round of the entire Kumbh-mela; if you ever hear—Whoosh! Whoosh!'

Without finishing the sentence, Bhootananda loudly clapped. Two crows had come and had sat on the branch of the nearby tree and were cawing loudly. Chased by Bhootananda, they flew away.

Bhootananda commented testily, 'Mother is not here, but her followers are very much around. All the black ones—crow or cuckoo—are Mother's followers. But have you noticed the difference in their cawing or cooing? Wait a little, sir. Since the followers are coming, they would not allow us to sit and talk in peace.'

Saying so, he got up and started climbing the tree with amazing alacrity. It was a huge old neem tree. I was completely taken aback. Bhootananda climbed a tree just to drive away the crows! It was a one-upmanship on Panchugopal's craziness!

Bhairavi was also looking up at the tree. Suddenly, a curse escaped her hushed voice, 'Death be on him!'

This was the first time I heard her voice. I did not know if this highland of Uttarpradesh ever witnessed such authentic Bengali rustic curse. I felt as if all the dry leaves made a murmuring sound in keeping with those four words from her lips.

I asked, not without a little fear, 'What's the matter?'

At my query, her angry face suddenly scintillated with a bright smile. She replied, 'Poison.'

Looking at my incredulous expression, she explained, 'Your Bhairav calls it the *charanamrita* of Mother Goddess Kali. The juice of neem leaves, Babu. It gives him a high.'

This was a total new revelation for me. I never knew that the juice of neem leaves can be made into an intoxicant. By then, Bhootananda had come down from the tree with a tin container in hand, which was overflowing with thick juice.

Bhairvi told me aside, in a low whispering tone, 'Do you now understand, Dadababu, why he told you that he cannot progress in his sadhana if he leaves this place?' She smiled bitterly, and a pathos spread through her entire face.

Bhootananda came and sat down with the box of tin. Then he said loudly, 'My dear Chandike, give me the piece of cloth. Let me strain the juice.'

Then he turned towards me and extolled the greatness of the Mother Goddess, 'Can't you see the manifestation of her *leela*? Otherwise, who would have kept this treasure of Mother's *charanamrita* for me to discover in this place? This is real nectar, babu. You are an educated city dweller. What can I tell you about its purity?'

I could correctly guess what he was leading to. He was subtly inviting me to taste his nectar. I dodged the hint and asked,

'How would you drink it? It must be very bitter.'

Bhootananda was already in a high spirit, 'Everything is bitter at the beginning. Then the sweetness follows. Just as joy follows sorrow. Otherwise, how will you digest joy?'

He again shouted, 'What are you doing, Chandike? I am asking for the strainer, but you don't seem to hear.'

This time, Chandike exploded. I had been noticing the symptoms for some time now. She threw the drumstick flowers on the ground and shouted, 'You are waxing eloquent about Kali in front of the gentleman. Aren't you ashamed? Shall I tell him your real nature?'

Bhootananda became completely nonplussed. He said placatingly, '*Arré*, what has come over you suddenly?'

Bhairavi chewed out the following words, 'Singing your glory, my dear. How long will you continue like this? You are extolling the virtue of your nectar, of the *charanamrita* of your Maa Kali. Can you tell me how I am going to cook the drumstick flower? Is there any damn thing at home?'

Byas! Bhootananda could take no more insult in front of a stranger. He jumped up, violently kicked away the tin of nectar, tied the red stole around his waist and shouted at the top of his voice, 'What? How dare you insult Maa Kali? I warn you, I'll murder you. I know your father's Keshto is speaking through you.'

Bhootananda called me as a witness, 'Warn her, Babu, otherwise I'll sacrifice her on the altar today.'

I did not know how to react. It was time for me to escape from here. How could I warn one party of the quarrel?

Who would think that it was Allahabad, the Kumbh-mela of Prayag? Who would say this was the ancient city of Pratishthanpur? I was hearing a typical conjugal quarrel of Bengal.

The furious appearance of the Bhairav was quite scary. But Chandrika (nee Chandike) was not at all cowed down. She took a couple of bold steps forward and said, 'My father's Keshto has the ability to do things, but your Goddess Kali is ungiving. Hence, you are also unmanly.'

I did not fully comprehend what the reference to 'father's Keshto' meant. But at this point, Bhairavi lifted her hands and tied her loose hair. She then addressed me, 'You know, Dadababu, before coming here, he persuaded me with a lot of bluff. When I asked, "How would we travel?" He said, "Don't worry, we would go without ticket. No one checks Kumbh pilgrims." "What would we eat?" "Lakhs of people will visit the mela, they will give donations of rice, dal and coins. Nothing to worry about it." And now? He lives here and keeps drinking his nectar. Never takes the trouble of going down and beg for alms. I have not eaten anything in the last two days. I have no means to light a fire in this chilly winter. And he boasts of the *leela* of Mother Kali.' Her voice croaked at this point.

Bhootananda could not bear such insinuation to his inability to feed his woman. It was an insult to his manhood, especially in front of an outsider like me. With his eyes blazing, he hurled the ultimate indignity, 'Such big words from a fallen woman like you! Are you my married wife whom I have pledged to feed twice a day? I have not taken any such vow before Maa Kali.'

Chandrika raised herself to her full height. Her eyes were also emitting fire. I felt as if an aura was radiating from her red-cloth-clad compact body. Her dark face looked like the hood of a black cobra, despite two days' starvation. Bhootananda could not bear to stand before such a fiery appearance. No man had ever been able to. He was looking for an escape route. Suddenly, he declared, 'I am leaving. You die here! Or you can gather people here with cymbals and drums to sing the name of your father's Keshto.'

With long and heavy strides, he really disappeared behind the trees. Strange fellow! Did not even think once that his invited guest was still standing here. However, I was suffering from a guilt conscience. Perhaps, I was part of the reason for this separation. Bhootananda would not have taken Bhairavi's insult to heart like this but for my presence.

As I started to make a move, I looked at Bhairavi and immediately came to a halt. Tears were streaming down her cheeks. I was desperately searching for a word of consolation when she spoke, 'Did you hear, Dadababu, how he disowned me? I have been with him for the last fourteen years. Maybe, there was no *saptapadi*, but I have walked a thousand steps with him. (Addressing her partner) I may not be your wife, but I am your Bhairavi. I am at your dharma, I am at your adharma too. I am with you in your happiness, I am with you in your distress too. (Addressing me again) So, is it proper on his part to spite me on the question of formal marriage?'

While saying so, her lips swelled and trembled. She resumed crying. I had nothing to say. But I could feel the pain and agony of a woman in this remote, solitary hillock of Kushi. It was as if I was watching a great drama of love playing out before me. I thought this was the ultimate reality of life—the pain of heart and the demand of stomach.

I looked around. The ashram of Bhootananda looked to me a poor man's hut in a Bengal village. A rustic dark housewife was standing with her head bent. At her feet, the uncooked drumstick flowers were strewn about. Perhaps, there were a number of girls and wives in this country in whose laps drumstick flowers were drying in absence of a drop of salt, a measure of oil and a plateful of accompanying rice. Starvation is a universal bane in my wretched land.

With a lot of hesitation, I took out some money from my pocket and called, 'Bhairavi!'

She removed the cover of her head and replied cheerfully, 'My name is not Bhairavi.'

'Is it Chandrika, then?'

'No, my name is Moila (a Bengali word that means darkish),' she flashed me a smile this time.

I said, 'Moila? What kind of name is this?'

'Because I was born dark, Dadababu, my parents would call me by this name. And it stuck.' She laughed again.

I was happy that the cloud had cleared a little. I extended the money and said, 'Buy some oil, salt and rice. Prepare drumstick flower curry today.'

She opened her palms and took the money unselfconsciously. Then she said something extraordinary, 'You have given a boon, Dadababu. Today, I will be able to serve him proper food. You do not know what great joy I derive out of it. I bow before you.'

I said doubtfully, 'How are you so sure that Bhootananda will come back?'

She replied confidently, 'Of course he will. Where will he go, leaving me behind? He says these things and threatens to leave only to hurt me, when he loses an argument.'

For a few moments, she brooded silently. I sensed she wanted to tell me something. I asked, 'Do you wish to say something, Moila?'

With uncharacteristic bashfulness, Bhairavi fixed her gaze at the horizon and said, 'Dadababu, please don't get angry with him. He is like that. Was a snake charmer, a daredevil in his youth. I am the daughter of a Vaishnav family. That is what he meant when he said "your father's Keshto". My father was a devotee of Lord Krishna. I tried to keep away from Bhootananda, but he used to pry around me. I was then a young girl in full bloom. If our eyes met, he used to say, "Moila, I am smitten by your dark beauty." I would get scared. One evening, he caught me in isolation and said, "Moila, I see manifestation of Mother Goddess Kali in you. I need you for my sadhana." Hearing this, I ran away in fear. Next day, when he repeated his desire I gathered courage and asked, "You see Maa Kali everywhere. People say you also see ghosts. Can you show me?"

He replied, "Of course I can. Come to Latai Chanditala tomorrow evening."

I did go, Dadababu, and he really showed me ghosts.'

I felt like laughing, but suppressed it and asked naively, 'Really? What did you see?'

'I don't know exactly what I saw or what he showed me. But I felt as if he controls the world. In the pitch of darkness, he was the lord over the gods and goddesses, the yakshas-yakshis and all. I also came under his spell, so much so that I eloped with him that night. I left behind my entire upbringing in a Vaishnavite culture. I was just sixteen. Since then, I have been with him.'

A perfect love story. I got up. She said, 'Please come again, Dadababu.'

As I was crossing the wood, someone coughed discreetly. Bhootananda. He asked, 'Are you leaving, Dadabhai?'

I suppressed my laughter and said, 'Yes, but what's the matter with you? You were supposed to have gone away.'

'What can I say? You have seen the real picture of my Bhairavi. She is like that. Please come again, I will tell you about my encounter with Maa Kali.'

I thanked my stars that he had not offered to show me ghosts.

I asked, 'Where is the well of Samudragupta that people talk about?'

He said, 'Do you see that fenced house? You will find the door to the well in its courtyard.'

I heaved a sigh a relief thinking of how Bhootananda would now go back to his 'ashram' and placate his Bhairavi with nice words. My mind gave a somersault in joy. A song started forming in my throat,

Let's go today under the huge sky.
A cosmic game is playing out.
Let's go to see it.

***

Reaching the fenced house, I found it quite crowded. Men and women were sitting around, talking to each other. Perhaps, they were taking rest. The painting that was adorning the temple in front was perhaps of Guru Nanak. The priest was Sikh, clad in white robe. He was distributing *charanamrita*. There was a staircase going down from the middle of the courtyard. I peeped in and found hundreds of people were climbing down swarmingly. A particular sight caught my attention. A hefty gentleman was simultaneously advancing and retreating in front of the stairs. A thin and bony woman was also matching his step similarly. Many people were deriding them as a source of fun. Obviously, they were afraid lest they die of asphyxiation inside the tunnel. I heard the man saying, 'God is not in my favour. How can I move ahead?' The woman, though clutching his hands, was calling him a 'coward.'

I did not have the mood to ponder over God's *leela*. Along with the crowd, I started climbing down the stairs.

Half-way through I realized that I had committed a great mistake. Even in this cold weather, I started sweating profusely. I was pasted against the person in front of me. Somebody else was pasted against my back. Our movement was involuntary. Even if one's last breath was squeezed out, one had to die standing. There was no room to even fall down. This was a death trap.

Suddenly, I felt a gust of cold wind on my body. Where was it coming from? Looking to my right, I found a ray of light coming from that side. Immediately, the huge flood of humanity started surging forward towards the light. Right from the torn cloth to soiled blanket to tridents, tongs, to the rustling sound of georgette saris, sweet tingling sound of gold ornaments and other jewellery to colourful dupattas and stoles to coat-pants—everything moved forward frantically. It seemed if one could complete the work here, the desired key to heaven would be in one's pocket.

It was impossible to stand on one place. I moved with the current. Everyone was chanting the name of Hanuman-ji. Turning right, I asked the next person, 'Is Hanuman-ji here?'

He said, '*Ji*, Babuji,' and immediately launched into a story, 'Once Hanuman-ji had to hide here, you know…' I was not interested in listening further. Surely, Samudragupta's well was constructed much after the time of the Ramayana. So, there could not be any history of Hanuman's hiding here.

However, I was surprised to notice that the man was trying to stand still. I asked, 'Why are you not moving forward?' He smiled and said, 'Do you want me to die?' And then he took out a coin from his pocket and threw it in a particular direction. I guessed that this was perhaps the hiding place of Hanuman-ji.

I moved forward. One had to admit that hard core pilgrims were much more patient, much more tolerant than I was. I saw a dim lamp, oily slab, a vermillion-smeared stone idol, pandas and paisas. A heady mix of devotion and piety.

As I turned back, I felt as if the buttons of my overcoat automatically gave way. A small hand crept in and was feeling my chest and belly. My God, my whole *amrita* was in a small leather purse on my chest. Someone was trying to pry it out. I caught hold of the hand hard forcefully. It was trying to wriggle out of my grip. I looked at the owner of the hand, and lo and behold, it was again the fallen woman of Khan-*pishi*, the man-stealer of Brajabala, the terror of the tents of Kumbh. The girl immediately changed tactics, hurled a stinging sidelong glance at me and said coyly, '*Chhor do na, chhoro mujhe babu* (Let me go; please let me go, babu).'

The moment I realized that I was holding the hand of a woman, my grip loosened. The bird of the cage was immediately liberated. There was a push and pull all around. I could hear her sarcastic laughter fading away. From the end of the tunnel, she looked back and hurled another sidelong glance at me. It seemed as if she was engaged in a deadly game.

I reached the end of the tunnel and cooled my body in the wind. Meanwhile, I had checked my chest and found the purse intact. I was relieved. That was my lifeline in the Kumbh-mela.

In front of me, there was the grey sky over the fort. Flakes of scarlet clouds were moving in a row. As a result, a crimson shade had fallen on the vast white stretch of sand. People moving far were looking like mysterious silhouettes. I also immersed myself in that light and shade, constantly making sure that the leather purse was there in its place. After all, it was *my* pitcher of nectar. I wandered among the crowd aimlessly for some time, like a shadow among the shadows. Gradually, a few stars appeared in the twilight sky. They were twinkling timidly among the dust and fog. The moon was also rising. Perhaps this is called dusk.

I moved to the south of the hillock and found a large ashram. It was brightly lit. A stage had been made on a raised platform. It was also garishly decorated. On the courtyard, a map of India had been artistically drawn with the help of small potted plants. In front of the entrance, I was asked to deposit my shoes to a custodian who gave me a ticket for it.

Two glamorously dressed young men were singing on the stage. The tune suggested that it was a bhajan, but the language was alien to me. The audience comprised more women than men. My sinner's eyes also took in the fact that a bevy of extremely beautiful women were around—all decked in gold and jewellery. The entire ashram was dazzling with colourful garments and ornaments.

A grave and irritated voice asked from nearby, 'Bangali-babu?'

As I turned to look at him, he instructed strictly, 'Drop the cigarette. The *maharaj*s are constantly coming and going.

If your smoke reaches their nostrils, you will be condemned to hell forever.'

A tall, fair, handsome man, clad in saffron was staring at me. His Hindi pronunciation had a hint of Punjabi accent. Thick curly hair covered his entire head. His mouth was covered in a cloth.

I immediately threw the cigarette away and asked, 'Is it a Sikh ashram?'

He was slightly mollified to see that I had readily obeyed him. He replied evenly, 'Not exactly. But a lot of Sikh devotees visit this ashram regularly. Moreover, the *maharaj*s do not like it at all. You people do not believe in any religion. How will it do if you smoke anytime anywhere?

'You people' meant who? Bengalis? I innocently asked, 'How can you say so, Maharaj?'

Now he sounded a little embarrassed. He replied less forcefully, 'So I hear, Babuji. I have never visited Calcutta, but heard that the menfolk there smoke a lot.'

There was no point protesting. I could raise counter-accusation, but how would it help? I changed the topic and asked, 'What's this ashram called, Maharaj?'

'Sadhubela Ashram. It is the most suitable ashram for the Hindus, Babuji. Its original location has now gone to Pakistan. So, currently it is located in Banaras. It is a very rich ashram having property worth lakhs of rupees. Hundreds of people are served prasad here everyday.'

There was no doubt that the wealth showed off, but the ashram lacked in charming smile and sweet disposition.

As I came out and collected my shoes, my eyes fell upon a signboard saying 'Reading Room'. I felt happy to see that scores of newspapers, magazines and journals were kept on a large table. Daily, weekly, monthly; political, cinema, literature—all were there. English, Hindi, Urdu, Tamil, Marathi, Oriya—all were lying side by side. But I could not find anything in Bengali, though I thoroughly searched the table. A little disappointed, I turned away when someone thrust a 'Visitor's Book' at me for signature. Why not? I signed my name in Bengali. This was not my protest at all. I had no bitterness in mind, I just wanted a little presence of my homeland, Bengal, in this Reading Room corner.

This time, I moved towards the north-west corner of the fair, which I had not seen so far. As I covered some distance negotiating the crowd, I found a large group of people being led by none other than Panchugopal. Seeing me, he shouted affably, 'There you are! Where have you been roaming all day, dear?'

I was a little flabbergasted, being suddenly accosted like this and asked, 'Where are you people going?'

Without caring to respond to my query, he turned towards Di'ma and said, 'Khurhi, here is your ward. You were anxious about his whereabouts. Now ask him.'

The entire women brigade of our ashram, at least fifteen in number, was out there. Lo and behold, even Khan-*pishi* was standing side by side with Panchu Baidyi. I was told that if two powerful entities come together, explosion is inevitable. But shawl-clad Khan-*pishi* was looking rather composed now. She only said, 'It is that boy, right?'

Someone else replied, 'Yes.'

Di'ma asked, 'Have you eaten anything throughout the day?'

I lied, 'Oh, yes.'

Panchugopal commented, 'If you have had your food, why is your face looking so pale?'

I replied, 'Oh, that's because I've been wandering a lot.'

This time Panchugopal exploded, 'Enough! You cannot bluff Panchu Baidyi. Must have fallen under the spell of a sorceress. There are quite a few around, you understand. She will show you her moon face and take your life. This is Kumbh-mela.'

Khan-*pishi* came to my rescue, 'Come on, let's go. I am shivering in cold. Tomorrow is a full-moon night. Perhaps, the chill will intensify. I don't know what will happen.'

Panchugopal dittoed her, 'Yes, let's go.' I felt the command was directed personally to me.

While walking side by side, I asked, 'Which are the places you visited?'

Panchugopal replied in undertone, 'Up to hell. Do the women have any sense?' Loudly, he said, 'We went to the Ramakrishna Ashram, Anandamoyee Ashram and others.'

We walked a few paces in silence. Then I heard Didima telling someone, 'What can I do if he had not eaten? Is it my job at home also and outside also to call people and serve them food? If you are so concerned, you could have insisted on his eating before going out.'

Well, the dialogue was directed to little Brajabala whom I had not noticed so far. Under the moonlight, her eyes looked full of indignation and pathos. The moment I caught her eyes, she drew the border of her sari and covered her face. She was still young and tender. Her heart bleeds for an itinerant vagabond like me. Perhaps, these are the emotions which still keep our humanity going.

I could not sleep properly throughout the night. Apart from the cold, there were constant coming and going of people and regular snatches of conversation. Next morning, there was the auspicious dip in the Sangam as a Purnima (full moon) ritual. And then there were a lot of singing both far and near. People were coming from other places throughout the night for availing the morning dip. In the scriptures and almanac, the auspicious moment had been flagmarked. If you missed the dip at the given moment, you would miss the ticket to heaven. I could feel that even Didima was restless. She was occasionally lapsing into drowsiness, then would try to keep awake by chanting the name of her God.

I dozed off in the small hours of the morning, but Panchugopal's racket jolted me awake: 'Get up, you all. No time to lose.' This was immediately echoed by a number of shouts through the tent:

'Oh Nanda, my son, don't go away leaving me behind.'

'Oh Aunty, where is your towel?'

'Oh Maa, I can't find the bel (wood-apple) leaves that I tied in your sari corner yesterday!'

'Oh Nanibala, don't forget to carry the bowl of sun-burnt rice.'

'Oh daughter-in-law, I told you repeatedly last night to tuck some vermilion in the corner of your sari. Did you do that? You are a married woman; during the dip in Sangam you are supposed to scatter some vermilion in the Ganga.'

Such ruckus was heard from every corner. Take this, take that. The old women were crying in anxiety and fear. Please hold my hand. The old men were groaning: 'Oh God, give me energy, give me strength to sustain it.'

Outside, the cold was almost unbearable. The extremely severe Northern wind was blowing. But there was no time to think or step back. Move, move. Ambrosia was flowing in the Sangam. Life and youth, thoughts and ideas, desire and demand—all these are floating in the celestial ambrosia. Move, move, you have to dip in that nectar.

'Get up Braja! Move, move. Pehlad, my grandson, my golden pet, move, move.'

'Khan-*pishi*, move, move.'

'O dear, hold me, my feet are trembling. Take me along.'

Panchugopal's loud and impatient voice was heard from outside, 'Start moving, all of you. Start.'

I was hearing everything. Still, I remained inert on the bed. Who had given such an irresistible call? Whose flute played such magic on everybody's mind? What was driving all these people to take a dip in the cold water in this terrible winter dawn? My mind was restless, but body still. I kept lying on the bed.

Suddenly, I heard Di'ma saying, 'Pehlad, call the boy.'

Prahlad shouted, 'Hello, brother, get up. Otherwise, all the efforts of so many days will go futile. Get up, get up!'

I did not respond. The cover of the tent was lifted. Everyone was going out. Suddenly, someone snatched the blanket away from me. It was Brajabala. Her face was bright with joy, eyes twinkling with expectation. She whispered urgently, 'Come on, quickly. Let's go.'

In a flash, she moved away walking in between Di'ma and Prahlad. But I could not forget the appeal of her innocent face. I got up and put on my overcoat. Even if I did not join in the dip, there was nothing wrong in going with all of them. There was no point lying in the empty ashram.

I met with Kotwalji outside and asked, 'Haven't you gone for the dip?'

He replied, 'Today is not our day, we shall take a dip on the new moon dawn. On that day, the auspicious *purna-kumbh* movement will arrive. Today also is not any less auspicious. But that day is marked for sadhus and renunciators.'

I went behind the tent at the tube-well space for washing my face. I thought it would be empty. But on reaching there, I was a little embarrassed. I saw the wife whose husband went missing from home standing there, staring at the distant sky with a vacant look. Her head cover had fallen off. The *anchal* of her sari had come loose. The forehead and the parting of her hair was smeared with vermilion. Tears were streaming down her eyes.

Behind her, the brother-in-law was standing quietly with a pale face and pained expression. Yesterday, when I saw them properly dressed for the occasion, I did not visualize this tragic moment. Only Brajabala told me that she did not talk to anyone. She was as if completely mute.

The sun was rising meanwhile. When on this golden morning, everyone was running for the nectar of life, these two persons were standing here in isolation. I did not know them. But I felt that an eternal tragedy was playing out before me.

My presence broke the spell. The lady cast a quick glance towards me and disappeared into the tent. The brother-in-law stood uncertainly for a few more moments with his head bent. Then he also followed suit.

Quickly washing my face, I came out. There were lakhs of people jostling against each other. Everyone wanted to move towards the Sangam. The endless stretch of sand was totally taken up by a sea of humanity. I lost my bearing. Which way to go? How to proceed? Sangam should be towards the south, but I found it impossible to proceed to the south. I crossed the bridge and alighted on the parade ground, below the embankment. Everyone was going towards the Sangam from this side also. Police had set up rows of ropes to control the movement. Volunteers were trying to guide the pilgrims. The sound of their shrill whistles was a pain to the ear. I was pushed by the jostling crowd towards a particular direction.

Mikes and bugles were giving out signals for the people to follow. The scout band was doing parade on the sand. It was rumoured that Prime Minister Jawaharlal Nehru was coming. On the way to the Kalyani Congress Session in West Bengal, he would visit the Kumbh-mela.

On the embankment, rows of elephants were moving majestically. Their howdahs were gorgeously decorated with zari and velvet cloth. Ash-smeared sadhus were seated on them. A bunch of girls were running towards them and shouting, 'Hey, Bhagwan! Hey Baba! Wait a little, please go slow.'

I asked a passer-by, 'What's happened? Why are they running after the elephants?'

I learnt that they would touch the body of the elephants and bow their heads to it. That would earn them a lot of piety.

What madness, I thought. Didn't they even have the fear of life? Is piety that important?

Suddenly, I was alarmed by the repeated warning, '*Hut jao, hut jao* (move aside, move aside).' As I stepped aside, I found a group of men clad in cloaks were marching ahead. Their clothes were soiled, their faces were dirty and, their hair was matted. Long hair and beard had covered their face in such a manner that it was difficult to recognize them as human beings. They were carrying long cloth-bags and walking forward briskly. A lot of men and women were running after them, touching their feet, putting alms on their cloth-bags and praying, 'Give me your blessings, Baba! Give me your blessings!' These were not riff-raff, but well-dressed men and women from wealthy families. Many of the women were wearing gold jewellery.

But the cloak-clad army was heartless and unkind. They did not know how to stop. One young woman with her head covered with the *anchal* of her expensive sari stood in front of a cloak-clad person with both her arms stretched out. He had to stop. But his feet were still moving like the 'left-right' parade of a soldier. There was no anger in his eyes that were covered by hair. It only showed eagerness to move ahead.

The woman took out her pretty handkerchief and removed a few rupees from inside it. She put it in the jhola of the sadhu and extended her palm to get something in return. The sadhu tore off a piece of his dirty dress and put it on her hand. Then he pushed her away and marched forward.

Many shouted, '*Mil gaya, mil gaya* (She has got it, got it)!'

I was totally confused. Who were these people? Where were they marching to? My query elicited a strange reply, 'They are great men. They would never stop in this life. Right from the day of their initiation, they have been marching forward. This is their sadhana.'

I did not know what to make out of this reply. I asked, 'Do they have a name?'

'Not that I know of.'

Before one could digest this information, there was another huge wave of people. I was also pushed forward toward the Sangam. Was it just the confluence of Ganga, Yamuna and Saraswati or the confluence of humankind too, I wondered. But there was not much time to wonder. The current drew me away, towards the river. A group of women were laughing, singing and surging forward. A few oldies were there, but mostly younger ones. Fair, snub-nosed, slit-eyed and thin-lipped. They were rather short in height, but were indomitable, like forest dwellers. Whenever you caught one's eyes, her face would brighten up with a smile. I took courage and asked one, 'Where are you coming from?'

She burst out laughing, like the members of Shyama's group and said, 'We are coming from Hardwar. You?'

I said, 'Bengal'.

'Calcutta?'

Again another fountain of laughter. The crowd also looked at us. A saffron-clad female *sadhika* offered an explanation, 'We are *avadhuts*. We have an ashram in Hardwar.'

Really? But I thought female *avadhuts* must always have a male counterpart. But who were the male *avadhuts* of so many women?

Move, move, move forward. There were rows of beggars on both sides of the path—healthy, sick, lame, deformed, blind. The soiled pieces of cloth spread in front of them were filling up with rice, dal, flour, coins, etc. In the midst of it, snake charmers had sat down with slimy serpents. Along with it, they had spread their wares on pieces of cloth—herbal leaves and grass of many variations. They were hawking their remedies on top of their voices.

The *hathyogis* had started demonstrating their formidable acrobatic skill. Someone was standing on his head, another lying on a bed of thorns with bare body. At one spot, a young boy of around ten years was lying on his back on a rack. A thin sharp trident had pierced his tongue. Water was streaming down his eyes and his body was trembling like a leaf in the wind. I was stricken by pain. What kind of religion was this that made a boy undergo such a cruel practice?

The next moment, I realized that it was not just religion. It was a sadhana of a different kind. It was a sadhana to fill up the stomach. People were throwing in money, amazed at his achievement. I noted that even in the midst of his great physical pain, his eyes were darting from people to people to gauge who was gifting what. The women stood surrounding him. Their motherly instinct felt pity for the boy.

But pity would not help. I threw a few coins on the cloth and moved on. As I reached near the river, I met with another disaster. A lot of mud had formed on the bank and men and women were pushing and pulling on that mud like buffaloes gone berserk. A little farther, any number of boats were manouvring for space on the Sangam. Barriers of ropes were put up to mark the specific area for the dip. Volunteers' whistles were constantly attracting the attention of the people. Banners were flying. The danger zone had been marked clearly. In your zeal to play with the blue water of the Yamuna you might cross the danger zone where certain death awaited you.

Amidst all this jostling, people were reveling too. Here was someone mirthfully throwing water on another. There was someone carrying another to the river.

An old man suddenly came near me and held both my hands, saying, 'Maharaj! Maharaj!'

I asked, 'What do you want me to do?'

He led me by the hand to the water and took a couple of dips in half-mud half-water, without ever letting me go. Once back on the bank, he laughed a toothless laugh and put his muddy hand on my head in benediction and said, 'Long live, son. I am scared of water, as I don't know swimming.'

Well, he earned his share of piety, but soiled my clothes. Of course, here nobody paid much attention to clothes. Everyone was semi-naked. I was particularly impressed by the Punjabi women. They were laughing and jumping in joy and shedding their salwar kameez without any inhibitions. Once their naked body adjusted with the chill of the water, they got busy enjoying natural water sports like swans.

A boatman was calling, 'Come over, two annas each. You will take a dip bang at the Sangam.' It was a large boat. Many people started climbing on to it. I also took the extended hand of the boatman and boarded it. Gradually the boat filled up completely, but the boatman was still shouting, '*Do anna, do anna.*' We all started clamouring for the boat to start. At one point when it seemed as if the boat would capsize, he started rowing it. Many of us were scared. But a few young suited-booted Punjabi young boys and girls were making merry. After some time, I realized that their laughter was propelled by fear. None of them knew how to swim. Hence, as the boat swirled off balance, they would clasp each other in fear and laugh. I could see a Bengali family also on the boat. Two young men and three middle-aged women. They had towels tied around the collars of their Alistair. The young men were even carrying cameras around their shoulders.

There were around thirty people in all on the boat. Among them, two very young girls seemed to be busy protecting a child. The girls were not expensively dressed, but they were wearing a lot of ornaments. There were gold ornaments on their wrists, neck, ears and nose. One of them was wearing a huge number of cut-glass bangles. But I could not gauge why they had brought the child along.

Just as there was a crowd of people on the shore, there was a crowd of boats on the water. Oar was hitting against oar, scull was hitting against scull. The prow of one boat was pushing against that of another, creating a ruckus.

The boatman said, 'Get down here, all of you.'

There was a storm of protest. Since we had hired the boat, we would go to the centre. No one got down. Everyone urged the boatman to move ahead further.

The Ganga and Yamuna were flowing side by side. Saffron and blue, two shades. One was going from North to South straight, the other was from West to South with a curve. One was blue with the pain of separated lovers from age to age. The other was saffron-coloured in the indifference of having achieved everything. One laughs a juvenile laugh, the other laughs like a mad woman. Yet both are always side by side, rushing towards the horizon for the same attraction. But where is the Saraswati, the third partner in the Sangam? It is said that she remains hidden.

Flower and wood-apple leaves were floating on the water. The vermillion offered by the women had made a portion of the water crimson-coloured.

Finally, it was time to take the dip. Everyone got rid of their clothes and dipped in the Ganga, firmly catching the boatman's hands. Among them there were a number of young, buxom North Indian women. The toothless old boatman helped them bathe, constantly chanting 'Hai Ram! Hai Ram!'

As everyone shedded their clothes, they looked at me suspiciously. Why was this idiot still standing fully clothed? Suddenly, I was brought to attention by the sound of hushed crying. Who was it? One of those two young girls, who had a few months old baby on her lap. The other with the cut-glass bangles was consoling her, '*Mat roh* (Don't cry)'. Though she was putting a brave front, her eyelids were also heavy with suppressed tears. It seemed that she was a little abashed also by their show of grief in the midst of all the exhilaration around. I was intrigued. When all the people were busy collecting the nectar of piety, why were these two young girls shrouded in sorrow?

They opened their bundles. There were clothes in them. One on top was a white muga silk dress. I was surprised to see a pair of gold bangles kept on it. It dazzled brightly as the morning rays of sun fell upon it.

Then the younger girl laid down the woollen-clad child on the deck of the boat. Immediately, the child started crying on top of its voice. The girl now broke down on the shoulder of the slightly elder one. Her head cover had come off. Her dry hair was flowing in the wind. Now her companion also joined in the weeping, though murmuring, 'Don't cry, Shivpiyani. Don't cry, my sister.' Nobody was paying any attention to them. It did not occur to anyone why they were not accompanied by a male companion. Everyone was busy with oneself.

Meanwhile, the child had brought its own right foot in its mouth and tumbled to one side. I felt concerned for the child's safety and picked it up on my lap. The girls looked at me in surprise. Teardrops were still lingering in their eyes.

I asked, 'Why have you put the child down like this?'

The companion of Shivpiyani replied, 'We want to bathe in the river.'

What madness! I was irritated and asked, 'But why the child?'

The companion said, 'He also needs to take a dip.'

My heart bled for the child. You have just arrived on this earth and already it has been decided that you need to earn piety.

I suggested, 'Why don't you take a dip and spare him?'

This turn of conversation seemed to have made both of them slightly embarrassed. After a few moments of silence, the companion offered an explanation, 'The child has lost its father. We have to keep him alive. How could we do it without bathing him in Ganga-ji.'

At these words, another wave of weeping came over Shivpiyani. Both of them held each other and proceeded towards the side of the boat. The companion turned back and told me, 'Let me help her take a dip. You…'

The rest remained untold. I was being requested to look after the child in the meantime. They went down into the water. The child had found a warm lap by this time. Not aware of the loss of his father, he revelled in the sunlight, thudding his tiny feet, raising his hands in the sky and emitting a lot of saliva on my face.

I had accompanied everyone here to see how the mad rush for taking the dip in the Ganga went. And from nowhere a child came and occupied my attention. I did not know who or how his departed father was. Seeing so much ornaments on her, I could not even imagine that the child's mother was a widow. Perhaps the gold was a kind of future security. Perhaps the longevity of this child would add to her security. Or maybe I was wrong. Maybe it was completely the propitious affection of a mother's heart to ensure that her son did not inherit the short span of life that his father had.

The two girls had got up from the water and changed their clothes. From their conversation, I learnt that they were sisters-in-law; they lived right in Allahabad city.

Putting on new clothes, Shivpiyani took out the flowers and bel leaves from her bundle and stretched her hands towards me. As I handed over the child, they undressed him and laid him down on the deck again. Then both of them brought river water in their palms and sprinkled it over him. A symbolical bath. Another round of shrill crying. Dressing him in warm clothes, she slipped both the bangles on the child's wrists and then without any hesitation handed it back to me. Then they threw down flowers, bel leaves and vermillion on the water. Suddenly, Shivpiyani took off both the gold bangles from her wrists and immersed them in the water. Her companion tried to dissuade her, but in vain.

The companion finally gave a pathetic smile and said affectionately, 'Crazy girl!'

Though she resisted the act, she had no regret for what the crazy girl had done. Shivpiyani looked at me with the hint of a smile and then asked her companion, 'Give the child to me.' Hearing this, I promptly handed over the child to her.

The boatman shouted, 'Get back into the boat, all of you. I have to make another trip.'

Many of my co-passengers were still in water. Particularly, the Sikh women were really enjoying themselves and were in no hurry to get up. Suddenly, someone tugged at my overcoat. Turning around, I found an elderly Sikh gentleman with flowing beard and hair cascading down his shoulder. He smiled mischievously and asked, 'You, Brother, why are you not taking a dip?'

I tried to evade the onslaught by weakly protesting, 'I am not well.'

But by then, he delighted himself by sprinkling some water on me, saying, 'One has to touch the water here.' Sensing fun, his female companion also sprinkled some water on me. My overcoat got wet and the cold water cut into my skin.

The boatman gave the final warning. 'I'll now start the boat.'

That resulted in another crowding, jostling, pushing and pulling. Returning to the shore, I saw Khan-*pishi* in the crowd. She had got her head tonsured and was looking like a mountainous male species. Even Prahlad and Didima's heads were also tonsured.

Prahlad first spotted me and shouted, 'Here, Dada! You seem to be enjoying the breeze of the Ganges. No bath? No shaving the head?'

I smiled and replied, 'No.'

Prahlad asked a strange question, 'Why? Have you not committed any sin?' As I had nothing to reply, I just smiled again.

He continued, 'Haven't you heard the couplet:

Tonsure your head in Prayag

Go on committing more sins.

Khan-*pishi* snorted through her nose angrily, 'What nonsense! How can you people talk rubbish standing by the sacred Sangam?'

Prahlad muttered under his breath, 'Couldn't find an opportunity of joining the palm together since morning, and she is talking of the sacred Sangam!'

I understood that by 'joining the palm together', he meant taking a puff of the ganja.

Shivpiyani and her companion stood for a while after

getting down from the boat. As I got down, the companion said, 'Goodbye (bidai)!'

I said, 'Goodbye!'

Shivpiyani shook the child and told him, 'Say goodbye'.

By this sudden shake, the child looked a bit surprised. Next moment, it threw its arms and feet around and uttered a few unintelligible syllables. Both the women laughed at the child's mischief and moved away.

I heaved a sigh and pushed off. Then I saw something terrible. That dangerous thief-woman, Brajabala's man-stealer, Khan-*pishi*'s home-wrecker was standing close to Khan-*pishi* herself. But what a metamorphosis. She had vermilion smeared all over her forehead. Her sari-blouse were wet with water. And she had a man with her, a sickly, dark and thin man, whom she was virtually dragging with her. She was telling him something and pouring water on his head with her palms cupped together. The man was receiving it in a docile manner and laughing out by the tickling coldness. There was no trace of that sidelong coquettish glance, no hint of that devastating crooked smile. She was as if a different person.

Suddenly the couple bumped with Khan-*pishi*. She turned her huge body with an angry look. I was apprehensive that a terrible brawl would ensue. But even Khan-*pishi* did not recognize her. Khan-*pishi*'s face broke into a tender smile. She asked,

'Who is this, daughter? Your husband?'

The thief-woman nodded and said, 'Yes.'

Khan-*pishi*'s eyes clouded with pain. She asked, 'Has he been suffering for long?'

The woman replied, 'Yes, for a long time.'

Khan-*pishi* looked at the man with deep empathy. Her eyes welled up with tears. She said, 'He will be all right, daughter, I tell you. You have taken so much trouble to bring him to the Sangam. I bless you, let the conch bangle on your wrist and the vermillion at the parting of your hair be permanent. Long live both of you.'

I did not know how much that Hindi-speaking woman understood of Khan-*pishi*'s blessings in Bengali. But my mind was filled with a sense of wonder. I bowed before the nobility of human hearts. I thought of that woman as a fallen being, always bent on sinning and pushing others to sin. But today she stood before me with the full glory of a propitious woman.

Pushing through the crowd, I climbed up on the embankment. A cavalry was marching forward. Nehru was coming. The crowd swelled up in anticipation of both a dip in Sangam and a peep at Nehru.

Suddenly I felt a cold touch on my shoulder. Startled, I jumped aside. The tail of a huge python had touched my neck. The owner of the snake put it round his own neck and reassured me, laughing and showing his large yellow teeth, '*Kuch dar nahi beta* (Nothing to fear, son). This is the garland of Lord Shiva.'

I was a bit pissed off. I said testily, 'Enough of Lord Shiva. Is there no other way to attract attention without setting a snake's tail on me?'

But he brushed aside my anger with total nonchalance. He was wearing a dirty saffron robe with numerous patches. There was some similarity with Bhootananda Bhairav in his appearance, what with long unkempt hair and beard. He was carrying a rather large cloth bag and a strange-looking staff. The zigzag shape of the stick almost resembled a snake.

Looking at my angry face, he gave a beatific smile and said, 'Look, Babuji. Whomever this snake had touched is blessed with a good fortune. I can see that you also have good days ahead.'

Having said so, he seriously started examining my forehead. I was impatient of such namby-pamby and made to leave. But he quickly blocked my way and said,

'Listen, son. Where are you going? You have a great fortune. I will bestow the prasad of Mahadev on you today.'

Saying so, he dipped his hand in his bag and brought out something in his fist, and said, 'Open your palm, son. Take it.'

I was apprehensive. I asked stubbornly, 'Fist show me what you have in your fist.'

He replied, 'Don't be cross, son. Accept it.'

He was a blackguard. I had to finally accept his offering. It was something small, hard and hairy.

I asked, 'What is this?'

He replied in a hushed voice, 'The horn of a jackal.'

I was flummoxed. I had seen horns of many quadrupeds, but never saw or heard of a jackal having a horn. Even if I temporarily suspended this question of gullibility, I still would not know how it could help me.

I asked, 'What shall I do with it?'

He laughed and said, 'You don't have to do anything, son. Just keep it with you. Everything else will be done by Lord Shiva. Usually jackals do not have horns. But one which gets the darshan of Lord Shiva, grows it. How does a jackal meet Lord Shiva? Only when He comes down to meet Devi Kalika in the jungle. A rare opportunity for a jackal to see Him.'

Well, all that was fine. But how could I claim a share of the sadhana that I had not gone through? Seeing my hesitation, the saffron-robed sadhu whispered in my ear, 'This gives you the occult power. The whole world will be at your feet. Your desired person will come to you and make you happy.'

I laughed out loud. For the first time, I laughed so heartily on the bank of the Yamuna. Using a charm? That too on the desired person? Some people had become mendicants in search of the desired person. Some were itinerant by realizing him/her, some without realizing. I did not know what was the appearance of the desired person. I had only hummed this song day and night—

I have roamed this way and that
At forests deep
The mind-bird kept singing,
I'm there within your mind.

What was the point of disturbing my beloved with the jackal's horn? I did not want to be the butt of her ridicule.

I told the robed solicitor, 'Sadhuji, I do not need this.'

But he was not to be shaken off so easily. With a serious face, he rolled his eyes and replied, 'My son, everything is not within your comprehension. This you will have to take. Don't hold it in the wind. Just put it in your pocket as a sacred thing. And reward me with whatever you can.'

I realized that rewarding him was the most important factor.

I asked, 'What will make you happy?'

He shut his eyes once and opened it again. Then he said, 'Not much. Give me just five rupees.'

I immediately extended his charm to him and assumed my urban personality. I sternly said, 'Take your thing back, Baba. I cannot buy it at five rupees.'

But he was quite adept in bargaining. He said, 'It is not buying or selling, son. It is a gift. Both from my side and yours. All right, give me two rupees.'

I still kept my hand extended and said, 'Leave me alone, Baba. I don't have two rupees even.'

'How much do you have, son?'

I had to take recourse to a lie and said, 'I just have four annas on me.'

There was an incredulous look in his eyes. Then he shook his head in despair and said, 'Then I have to take it back.'

I was relieved. As I made a move to put it back on his palm, he said thoughtfully, 'But how can I take back something I have already gifted? All right, give me the four annas. This piece was destined for you only.'

I was amused by now and thought why not take the bargain to its logical end. I said, 'But if I give away all the four annas, how will I manage? Take two annas, Baba.'

This time he was dumbstruck. Perhaps he never imagined that he would encounter such a hard nut in a pilgrim's place. He turned a little morose. I put the two annas and kept the jackal's horn in my pocket. As I started to move away, he entreated, 'Babuji, at least treat me to a glass of tea. What else can I ask for?'

Now his real self was revealing itself. I could not overlook and neglect it. I said, 'Come on, I will get you tea.'

While he was sipping the tea, I said, 'Keep your charm to yourself. But you don't have to return the two annas.'

He was blowing his breath to cool the hot tea. He said, 'Oh no, I can't take that thing back.'

This was the ethos of humanity. One would be broken, but won't bend. His temptation of the occult power could not make me a convert, but his honesty did. After the tea was over, I put two annas more on his palm and said, 'Bye, Sadhuji.' Before the smile of gratitude could form on his lips, I merged with the crowd.

In the crowd, I met with Hriday's mother. She saw me and caught hold of my hand. I was tired of roaming around and was proceeding towards the ashram for a little rest.

There was a sadhu sitting in front of Hriday's mother.

I asked, 'What are you doing?'

She said, 'I was just listening to some nice discourse from the Babaji. He speaks very well. He says, if the debtor turns his face and walks away, the debtee laughs. You just laugh and move around and enjoy. No one can pay the debt of a mother. When you die, your son will put fire in your mouth and cry. He will then curse himself thinking why he has not paid the mother's debt.'

Hriday's mother laughed. That laughter touched her wonder-struck eyes behind the thick and cracked lenses. She told the sadhu, 'All right, Babaji. Bye for today. I will come again tomorrow. Please find out a good Brahmin for me. I will feed him tomorrow.'

The sadhu was lean and thin, with a huge lot of matted hair. But even in this cold weather, he was naked, beyond a short brief (koupin).

He said, 'That's great. I am a Brahmin. So, your problem is solved.'

I said, 'Shall I make a move?'

But Hriday's mother did not let go of my hand. She said, 'Why should you leave? Come with me. Let us feed the sadhuji.'

I tagged along. I was not much curious, but a bit apprehensive about what Hriday's mother could afford to give the sadhu?'

There was an eating house nearby. The shopkeeper was not a local person. There was not much of a crowd in the shop. Large brasswares contained different kinds of sweetmeats. Puris were also being fried fresh. Hriday's mother took some water from the shop and sprinkled it on the earth. Then she wiped the spot with the *anchal* of her own sari and invited the sadhu, 'Come, sit here, Baba.'

The sadhu sat down and asked playfully, 'How much can you feed me, Mother?'

Hriday's mother replied, 'As much as you can eat.'

The she asked the shopkeeper, 'Give the sadhu all the items you have—puri, sandesh, peda, everything.'

After a few minutes, I grew more apprehensive. The fellow would not stop. The more he was eating, the more Hriday's mother kept looking at him with spellbound eyes. I was apprehensive because I was not sure if she could pay the huge bill. Even my sinful mind thought if Hriday's mother had dragged me into it with some purpose.

Even the shopkeeper was in some doubt. He asked, 'Should I give more, Mataji?'

Hriday's mother said without the least concern, 'Of course. Please keep supplying as long as he can eat. Is there more pleasure than in feeding someone, dear?'

This last question was addressed to me. I never felt so helpless in life. I was fidgeting with the purse in my pocket. The shopkeeper was spying at my cloth bag doubtfully.

The one who was eating and the one who was feeding were totally oblivious of any further repercussions. It is the shopkeeper and I who were doubting Thomases.

At one point, the shopkeeper announced, 'All my stock of food is exhausted. Now, you pay and look for another shop.'

Hriday's mother asked, 'Baba, would you like to eat anything more?'

The sadhu drank some water, wiped his mouth, burped contentedly and said, 'No, I am satiated.'

Hriday's mother told the sadhu, 'Nobody is happy with me. I am sort of unwanted. If you are happy, bless me.' Saying so, she bowed at the feet of the sadhu.

The sadhu said, 'Let there be joy in your mind.'

Once he left, Hriday's mother asked the shopkeeper, 'How much do I owe you, son?'

The shopkeeper said, 'I have not taken the small items into account. Still it has come to nineteen rupees and three annas.'

Hriday's mother looked at me once. Then she removed a dirty bundle from her waist and started counting the soiled and folded currency notes, as well as the coins. Whatever balance remained, she put it back in her small bundle and handed over the rest to the shopkeeper.

I was totally transfixed there, so was the shopkeeper. He took the money, did not even count it and looked at her as if he was having a 'Devi darshan' (Mother Goddess herself).

Hriday's mother looked at me. There were tears in her eyes, but smile on her face. Then she looked at the crowd outside and said, 'A weight of stone has been lifted today from my chest. Let there be joy in my heart. Let there be joy all around.' Driven by a tremendous emotion, Hriday's mother disappeared in the crowd, without even looking back at me.

I stood there with my head bowed down. She crushed all my mundane fear, my apprehension about payment, my doubt about her action as well as that of the sadhu. I did not have the kind of faith or devotion that Hriday's mother had. Perhaps this was called self-hypnotism. With the power of her faith and devotion, she demolished all that I stand for—my urban vanity and self-delusion.

***

The day passed in mad rush. Everyone dipped in the Sangam to their hearts' content. I would not know what nectar flew there today. I could not even begin to guess why everyone was feeling so happy about the bath. True, I had not come to Kumbh-mela to realize God. I was here to observe humanity, to dive deep into their minds. At this moment, even I felt as if my heart was full, there was no space even for taking a deep breath.

The sun had bent towards the western sky. Ideally, it was time to go back to the ashram and eat my meal. But my hunger had somewhat been blunted. Although I could visualize the anguished face of Brajabala, I decided not to return now. My legs took me towards the river where both the people and the boats had started thinning out.

Suddenly, my feet got stuck into something. I looked down and found a handicapped man had caught my feet. Thinking that it must be a beggar, I got a little peeved. As I was about to chastise him, he smiled. Lo and behold! It was Balaram.

Before I could say anything, he started singing full-throatedly, like a man possessed:

Who are you, oh mad fellow?
Feels like I know you from long past,
Oh mad fellow!

His resounding tone touched the sky. I felt there was a flood of water in my heart held back by a dam. It opened up and Balaram started rowing his boat in that river. I was not mad, it is Balaram who was mad. A few curious men and women were observing us. A little embarrassed, I said, 'Listen, Balaram!'

But Balaram kept on singing,

Was sitting with my heart open,
Today you blessed me,
Oh mad fellow!
Howsoever soot and dust you cover yourself with,
Whatever may be your disguise,
You won't be able to give me the slip,
Oh mad fellow!

I was quite moved by seeing Balaram's exuberance in finding me. But there were onlookers and I am a private person. So, I again called, 'Balaram!'

Balaram laughed like a drunk person and said, 'Yes, my guru.'

I said, 'There is a crowd.'

'Ok. Then let's go to wherever you were going. But I am not letting you go anywhere without me.'

'Near the Yamuna.'

Even before I could complete the sentence, he said, 'Excellent choice. Let's go.'

He dragged himself forward, supporting on his two hands, as if he was my guide. Every effort of his movement made me feel pained. Reaching the stretch of sand by the river, he uncoiled the towel from his head and stretched it on the ground, 'Sit down here, my guru.'

I was further embarrassed by his attention and said, 'The towel is not necessary.'

He immediately broke into another song:

If you do not want to sit on the ground, my love
Sit at the middle of my heart.'

I sat down. Balaram mused, 'I have never come to the bank of the Yamuna like this. Since I am here today, let me sing a few lines, if you permit, my guru.'

I said, 'Go ahead.'

At once, Balaram turned his face to the river and sang out in a sweet strain:

Yamuna, oh Yamuna
Are you the same river
On whose shore the Blue God played?
Where is that Chandravali,
Where is that dalliance in water
Where is Rai Binodini on Shyam's left?

Balaram returned Yamuna to her ancient glory. A part of the river suddenly turned crimson by the reflection of the setting sun.

Balaram looked at my face and said, 'This is the water that turned blue due to the tears of separation. I wonder, if the flute of the Blue God still plays out? If the anklets of Radha's feet still keep beat to that sound?'

After this philosophical observation, he laughed loudly and self-contentedly.

But suddenly he asked something, as if with a hurt sentiment, 'Sitting on the bank on the Yamuna, let me ask you something, my Guru. I know you have met a thousand souls here, but how could you forget me altogether?'

I reassured him, 'No, I have not forgotten. But I do not know where your ashram is.'

He said, 'It is just near the fort. The ashram of Baba Nandagopal Madhavacharya. You must come today. I am not alone, many people there are waiting for you.'

I was intrigued and asked, 'Who are you talking about—Lakshmidasi?"

He smiled, 'Yes, of course, there is Nakkidasi. But there are others too.'

I could not refuse. A light shadow of dusk had fallen on the water of the Kalindi. The dark shadow of the fort was dancing on the waves. At the corner of the Sangam, a temporary tower had been constructed with all the pomp and splendour. It was meant for the royal guests. Ordinary people could take a tour of the tower paying four annas. By the side of the tower, Balaram and I moved along making path through the crowd.

Light was gradually coming up in the shops, full of alluring wares. What particularly attracted my attention were heaps of glass bangles of many colours and many splendours. Around them were seated girls and women. Their laughter and animated conversations had made the fair more lively. I had heard that it was a custom in north India that during all festivities, social or religious, every woman wore numerous glass bangles, right from the super-rich to the ordinary. Those who were a little more fashionable would put a string of colourful beads around their necks. Heaps of multicoloured beads were on display. The potters of Azamgarh had set shop with varieties of earthwares—flower vase, teapot, even ashtrays for modern babus and ganja chillums for the rasikas.

My mind and legs sought to move in that direction. But I could not leave Balaram alone.

Even in his tiring effort to keep pace with me, he was humming a song. At one point, he asked, 'Guru, may I ask something?'

'What?'

'Why is your face looking pale? Even physically you have pulled down a bit? Are you living in discomfort?'

One whose whole life was full of discomfort was enquiring after my comfort! But I had no doubt about Balaram's keen power of observation. He had microscope in his eyes and he observed everything closely through it.

I replied casually, 'The whole day passes by roaming through the fair. Perhaps that's why—'

Balaram interrupted, 'It's because you are alone. If you had a companion, she would have looked after your comfort. Take care, guru. You will face big trouble if you fall sick in this far-off place.'

Led by Balaram, we were now walking through a narrow lane between two rows of tents. The sound of drums and cymbals were heard. A Bengali kirtan was being sung with a lot of gusto somewhere nearby.

We stopped in front of a tent. A woman was waiting in the semi dark area just outside the screen of the tent. Balaram tried to say something, perhaps an excuse for his delay, but she cast an angry glance and went inside the tent.

It was Lakshmidasi. Balaram lowered his voice and said, 'She is cross with me, but has not recognized you.'

I was thinking how the middle-aged singer could still display such fire of passion in her eyes.

As we entered the lighted area, she saw me and came running, saying 'My guru, so you remember us at last!'

Balaram tried to say placatingly, 'Did he remember by himself? I did meditation and sent vibes through air so that he remembers.'

Lakshmidasi did not even look at him. She folded her hands and said, 'Come inside, Thakur. You have to be with us for sometime. Won't let you go easily.'

I followed her and Balaram through the tent to a courtyard. A durrie was laid out on the floor. On the eastern side there was a low brass palanquin in which a one-foot-long Radha-Krishna joint idol was kept. In front of the image, a few *namavali*-clad men were singing the name of Lord Krishna swaying their bodies right and left. The drums and cymbals were keeping the beat with the rhythm of the song. One was standing and swaying in ecstasy. There was no electric light here. Only a petromax was burning. A few kerosene lamps were also burning inside the tents and in the cottages with acquatic grass awning.

Seeing me, even the singers missed a beat or two. Actually, my presence was a little incongruous there. The Vaishnavite sadhus watched me with large, curious eyes. I had seen a few of them with Lakshmidasi at the Allahabad station. Their faces had a stamp of rural poverty. I realized that an urban visitor like me was quite unexpected in this lowly ashram.

We crossed the congregation and went inside a thatched hut a little farther. Lakshmi spread a durrie and asked me to sit.

Balaram turned to Lakshmi and said, 'The face of our Thakur looks a little pale, as if he has been starving. Go Nakkithakrun, bring a little of Radhamadhav's prasad.'

I objected, 'That's not necessary, Balaram.'

But by that time, Balaram had started singing to himself:

Let's go, my mind,
Let's search for the God inside.
But, as you move, He also moves
So, it is a journey day and night.

Meanwhile, Lakshmidasi appeared with two pots of water in her hand. Her eyes were fixed on Balaram. I noticed that she became totally oblivious of my presence and was listening to Balaram's song, as if mesmerized. Once the song was over, Balaram looked up. At once, Lakshmidasi averted her eyes and put the two tumblers in front of us. Then she brought two plates made of sal leaves on which there were khichri, fried brinjal, cabbage curry and even a piece of sweet.

Balaram said happily, 'Me too? You served me food along with Thakur?'

Lakshmidasi addressed me, 'Please eat, Thakur,' but did not fail to look at Balaram in a side-long glance. I realized that even in his wretched existence, Balaram had a cover of safety and security. When I first saw him, I thought he was a mere beggar. Then I found out that he was the lead singer of an *akhra*. Now I found that there was an affectionate touch of someone in what he ate, what he wore and where he slept. I found the intimation of wisdom and devotion in Balaram's words and songs. Now, in Lakshmidasi's conduct I discovered the other side—love.

Suddenly, Lakshmidasi said, 'Thakur, I have a complaint. You will have to pronounce justice.'

Justice? No one had ever given me such an onerous responsibility.

Balaram started laughing uncontrollably. He said, 'All right. In every case, there is an accuser and an accused. The accused also gets a chance to reply. Please remember that, Thakur!'

Lakshmidasi complained, 'Look at him. And look at this huge mela. It is a death trap, with thousands of people, elephants, horses, tongas and what not. And this man, with his limited capacity of movement, goes out every now and then. If some mishap happens, what will I do, Thakur?'

Lakshmidasi looked at me with tearful eyes. It was true that Balaram was handicapped and there was lurking danger for him at every step in the fair.

But Balaram was unmoved. He smiled indulgently and said, 'Thakur, now listen to my submission. I am born lame. Nakkidasi did not want to bring me here. I almost forced myself into the group. But now that I am here, how can I keep sitting in the *akhra*? So many things to see, Thakur. You know it better than me. So, I thought I would move around as much as I can.'

He also had a point. Before the judge in me could take a stand, Lakshmidasi asked, 'If some mishap happens, then my *akhra* will plunge into darkness. Radhamadhav will not be satisfied by anybody else's song.'

I was totally ignorant of Radhamadhav's appreciation of music. But I could see that if anything happened to Balaram, a curtain of darkness would come down to someone's heart.

Balaram now addressed her directly and said, 'Nakkidasi, there are thousands of people outside. The Yamuna is flowing with warbling sound. He is also waiting there with his ears pricked. Don't you want me to sing for the real Him! Saying so, he sang out blithely:

I am there where you are!
I've no other furtile thought in mind.
If you summon, the doors open automatically
Then I dance at the tune of your breeze.

Byas! All Lakshmidasi's complaints were gone. She was looking at him and listening to his song spellbound. I wondered at the ways of the world thinking that a wretched lame fellow could create such ripples in the heart of a woman. Strange were the ways of the heart!

It was Balaram who broke the trance of Lakshmidasi, saying, 'Now that the Thakur is here, go ahead and make the request that you have been telling me all along.'

Lakshmidasi entreated, 'Yes, Thakur. I want to listen to a song by your Rabi Baul of Bengal.'

I was quite taken aback. One, I was not a singer at all. Two, how would Tagore's sophisticated lyric communicate to these people? And yet, Nandalal Bose's painting of Tagore as a *baul* flashed across my mind's eye.

The intensity of both Balaram's and Lakshmidasi's desire swept away my hesitation. Forgetting all my infirmity and failure, I started singing wholeheartedly:

My mind says, I want Him
Whom I have not realized
Amidst all the gifts that I got
An agony of deprivation rings in my mind
He is not here, no, not here

The star of the evening fades
To shine in the star of the morning
It says, let me go, friend, let me go.

Balaram bent down at my feet, saying, 'Such a wonderful song! You have all along been deceiving me, Thakur!'

Lakshmidasi's eyes were full of tears. I could not even imagine that Tagore's lyric and tune could move this motley group of uneducated rustic people to such a great extent. Suddenly, I found that there was a small crowd of listeners at the door. It was a moment of great embarrassment for me. Somebody even said loudly, 'An encore please!'

I thought it was time to leave. I jumped up, saying, 'Balaram, no more today. Maybe I will sing some other day.'

Balaram agreed, 'All right, I will not detain you any more, lest Nakkidasi thinks of making you the lead singer of her *akhra*.'

He was always full of zests for life.

I said, 'Please do not bother to come with me. I can find my way out.'

Balaram smiled his usual smile and said, 'But I have to lead you where you need to go now.'

'Where?'

He did not reply, but exchanged a meaningful smile with Lakshmidasi. Then he said, 'Come with me. I have been asked everyday where is your Thakur. I couldn't reply. Today I will show you off.'

Coming out of the tent, I found that the whole Kumbh-mela was flooded with moonlight. A huge full moon had risen in the western sky.

I told Balaram, 'Now I don't feel like going to another *akhra*, Balaram.'

He said, 'We are not going to an *akhra*, Thakur. We are going somewhere else.'

'Who is there?'

'You will see for yourself'—was his mysterious reply.

I had to tag along, for I realized that my refusal to go would be Balaram's loss of face. He must have committed something to someone.

We moved along the wall of the fort. Rows of tents were there, but since there were less shops in this area, the crowd was also less there. We stopped in front of a tent under a tree. A free space in front of the tent was covered by a canopy. A hurricane was burning. Under its light, I saw a woman making rotis on a baking pan and another was rolling the dough on a saucer.

Both the women turned towards us simultaneously. At once, there was giggling. I was startled to see that it was Shyama. The pan came down from the woven with a thud. Shyama's face looked reddened by the burning oven. Before I could react, Balaram said, 'Every day she asks me where is that babu of yours. So today, I thought I should quench her curiosity.'

Shyama's quick glances matched her coquettish laughter. Was there a little taunt also in it? Was she trying to tell me, 'Well, you had to come after all!'

I was temporarily transfixed there. But then I gathered myself and looked at her. By that time she had stood up. She was meticulously dressed in a silk sari. A woolen scarf was carelessly hanging from her neck. Her slanted eyes showed sharp curiosity. The crooked smile on her lips tried to be smart, but turned a little bashful in spite of herself. Gold ornaments were dazzling on her hands and neck. She fixed me in such a stare that I could not even avert my eyes.

Shyama quickly pushed the small charpoy on which she was sitting towards me and said, 'Sit down, please.' Her companion-cum-maid blurted out playfully, 'Hai Ram!'

I was still unable to get rid of my diffidence. I asked, 'Where are the others?'

She asked, 'Who are you talking about?'

I said, 'Your co-wives, husband and all?'

Shyama raised her eyebrows and asked, 'Is it forbidden to sit if they are not around?'

Her tone turned sarcastic. The smile on her face was about to fade. Her intense gaze was as if trying to search my soul.

I quickly said, 'No, nothing like that. I was just asking.'

Shyama said, 'Then why are you looking *naraj* (cross)?'

I was not cross. I was just uneasy. My so-called civilized mind dictated that it was not proper to visit a stranger woman in her tent at night. Balaram did not care for, nor did he understand, such norms. But I had a problem of propriety.

Still I sat down. But I had a foreboding about Shyama's conduct. If she laughed in gay abandon and made merry with her companions at my cost, I could understand that.

But if she looked at me searchingly without batting an eyelid for long, I felt uneasy.

The companion-cum-maid commented in a hushed but bantering tone, 'So much for making roti this night.'

Shyama immediately tugged at the braid of her hair. The girl managed to keep her balance and said, 'Ooof! Why don't you pull your own hair rather than mine?'

I could see that the girl was not just a maid, but a sort of companion in bantering and a Woman Friday too. But the servant-girl's bantering worked. Shyama again sat down before the oven.

Balaram's overflowing emotion refused to remain in further check. He started humming a song to himself:

I had so much to say
But no words came to my lips,
Oh friend, time flies
Chest explodes, but the mouth remains mute.

They might not have understood the language of Balaram's song. I did. It was slightly embarrassing. To ease the tension, I raised my face to say something. Shyama also raised her face at the same moment. Both of us stopped short.

Then Shyama asked, 'You were saying something.'

I said, 'You too.'

She replied, 'I was asking where are you putting up. Which ashram?'

I told her.

Shyama then went ahead to enquire everything in detail, like whether the ashram was good, what was the food like, which were the places I visited, etc. As I was replying as faithfully as possible, she was looking at me with sidelong glances and smiling her trademark smile. Then she suddenly commented, '*Ajeeb aadmi*. You are a strange person!'

'Why do you say so?'

'I don't know. Did I give you much trouble in the train the other day?'

I asked, 'Have you summoned me for that?'

She said bashfully, '*Hat*!'—which may mean 'nonsense' or 'get lost'.

I got up and said, 'Let me take your leave today.'

Shyama quickly asked, 'Will you come again tomorrow?'

I should have asked why, but could not muster courage to do so. I just said lamely, 'Will try.'

I came out of the hut. Balaram followed me. He was still muttering a song. The light of the hurricane inside was immediately forgotten. The full moon light of the month of Magha flooded the entire landscape.

I heard Shyama's hushed call from behind, 'Listen.'

I looked back. The blue moonlight was shining on her subdued rust-coloured silk sari. The silver-coloured scarf also dazzled under the moonlight. She came near me and asked, 'Were you angry with me that day?'

I could see an anguished expression on her face. Perhaps, unknowingly, I had knocked at the door that she had closed with so much bitter pain. It was my mistake.

I said, 'No, I was not angry at all.'

'*Sach*? Are you telling the truth?' Her face betrayed doubt and suspicion.

I reassured her, 'Why should I lie? I am telling you the truth.'

This time, gratitude showed in her eyes along with the customary laughter. She said, 'Please come tomorrow. Same time!'

Our eyes met. I could see appeal in her eyes along with the request.

I came out without committing anything. I did not forget that Balaram was with me. Shyama was not a fallen woman. She was the young wife of an octogenarian *kuleen* fellow. In her heart, the spark of a thousand thunders was lying dormant. In a festive night it tended to burst out like a colourful cracker at the open sky, though her life was doomed to darkness. That is why she was different in all situations.

Balaram suddenly asked out of the blue, 'Is the Thakur cross with me?'

I replied briefly, 'No.'

'Then may I dare tell you something?'

'Yes, of course.'

'You must hook up with a guru.'

'Guru? Why should I need a guru?'

Balaram said, 'Can there be any sadhana without a guru? From our birth to our death, many gurus cross our path. But they would not let you know. You have to recognize one.'

He started humming:

Oh, my mind, whom do you bow down to as guru?
There is guru inside you, guru outside you
Gurus are numerous.

Then he said, 'One of the gurus is your woman companion, your female counterpart. Do you understand? Without this guru, everything is in disarray.' He laughed out. I perhaps became a little unmindful. Then I asked him,

'Have you got your guru, Balaram?'

'Yes, Thakur.'

'Who is that guru?'

'One who makes me cry by crying herself.' He wiped his tears.

I could see he was referring to Lakshmidasi. I left him and walked away. At last my Sangam dip happened in the tears of Balaram. I stopped near the water. A hundred faces came flocking around before me. They all got submerged in the procession of the lakhs of faces in the Kumbh-mela. I had met so many gurus here—on the road, in the stretch of sand, in cottages, slums, buildings, at home and the world. I bowed before these numerous gurus.

***

Next evening, I could not go to meet Balaram or Shyama. Not that I did not want to, but there were quite a few spots to visit yet. In the evening when I was returning from the other side of the Yamuna by a boat, there was suddenly a storm and a thunder shower. The heart of the Yamuna was cleaved by repeated lightning. Great waves rose. The boat started swaying. A darkness enveloped all around like a deluge. I felt like singing aloud:

> *Unmad pavaney Yamuna tarjita*
> *Ghana ghana garjita meha,*
> *Damakat vidyut pathataru lunthita*
> *Tharathar kampita deha.*

Finally, when the boat managed to cast anchor at the bank of Jhusi, I was thoroughly soaked. As such, it was a very cold evening. Over and above, I was wearing an overcoat which was now totally wet. To cap it all, it was still raining hard. My teeth were chattering in cold, my knees were knocking at each other. Everyone was running in search of shelter, both men and beasts. I did not know how I managed to reach the ashram.

It rained through the night. In the morning, it was heard that a sadhu had died of cold the previous night. He was perhaps the first victim of the cold wave. A little later, a terrible cold wave came upon the mela like a curse. This was happening throughout Uttar Pradesh. The mela started breaking up.

The sadhus who set up their lodgings under the open sky started running towards the city with their *lota-kambal* (the metal pot and the blanket). Those whose makeshift shelters or weak tents were ravaged by last night's storm, salvaged as much material as they could and decided to go back home. Everywhere there was an atmosphere of listless abandoning. I never imagined how a sheer cold wave could wreack such havoc. Now, everyone was craving for a little fire. Fuelwood was not only selling at a premium, but was pilfered and snatched. The nomadic men and women around Allahabad suddenly found a vocation. They would gather wood from the jungle and sell it at the fair. There was almost a stampede over the fuelwood.

The rich ashrams were in a better position. They had enough food and firewood. The Nagas in these ashrams were still moving around naked. As such, their tents were warm and in any case, they never cared for the cold.

I could not go out of our ashram for three days. One, it was very cold and there was nowhere to go. Two, my wet overcoat was not likely to dry up before three months. Already it was weighing around three *maunds*. Suddenly, I heard a commotion in front of our ashram. I came out and found that two persons had caught hold of a sadhu who in his turn was holding a stack of dry wood. What was the matter? It seemed the sadhu had stolen the pieces of wood from the shop of those two men. The sadhu refused to be taken to the police station and was hurling chosen curses at those two men. At last, the two men gave up and decided to give him a beating. The fellow bore all those beatings with a smiling face and said at last, 'You hit me. No problem. *Magar lakri nei denge* (But I would not give up the pieces of wood).' Then he left laughing.

One day, I went to the city of Allahabad and visited Anand Bhavan and the ashram of Sage Bhardwaj. I had a small work in the post office, where I bumped into an old friend. He was a respected professor at the Allahabad University. To spend time with him, I kept visiting the city regularly for a few days.

Then I got an invitation to visit the fort and take a tour inside it. The common public are forbidden to enter that area. The mansion inside the fort was rose-coloured. There was an external wall to protect it. The door in the wall was always closed. I was told that the inner chamber of the mansion was packed with gunpowder. For security reasons, even ordinary staff members of the fort were also not allowed in. I walked around the terrace and the bay window. There was no door to enter the bay window. There never was. Heavy velvet screens used to hang there. The wind from the Sangam would sway the screens and enter the mansion. The chandelier of cut glass used to make tinkling sound. It is in this mansion that Emperor Akbar used to hold his court.

I came out. On the eastern side of the mansion, there was a double-storied building, behind which was a wall surrounded by bushes. Beyond that, the Ganga was flowing. At one spot, I noticed a huge banyan tree. The original tree was almost invisible, because hundreds of aerial roots had created a number of separate trees. The deep grove of the trees was semi-dark. At its base, a portion of the ground had been cleaned and mopped. A signboard announced its name 'Akshaybat' (the banyan tree that never perishes). So, this was the oldest banyan tree in north India.

On the accessible side of the fort where numerous gods and goddesses reside in an underground chamber, there was another banyan tree. The pandas claim that one to be the original Akshaybat. But history does not support this claim. At one time, newspapers also exposed this tree as an artificial one, made by the pandas only to earn money. Shri Shivnath Katju conducted a research on this issue and concluded that the banyan tree standing in isolation outside the rampart was the original Akshaybat. If you stand on it, you could see the confluence of Ganga and Yamuna below. Beyond that, you would find an ocean of people and tents.

Once, a thousand Hindus turned martyrs by jumping down on the Sangam from this tree. Historian Abdul Kader Badauni, who was a contemporary of Huen-Tsang and Al-Beruni has documented this incident in detail. It happened during the reign of Akbar. Even Tulsidas has written about it in his *Ramcharitmanas* in the following lines:

Sangam simhasanu sudhi soha,
Chhatra akshaybat munimon moha.
Pujahin Madhava pad jaljata,
Parasi akshaybot harakshmahin gata.

As I looked at the sand-band on the far side of the Sangam, I wondered where Emperor Harshvardhan used to sit with the crown on his head. Where was his five-yearly great congregations used to be held where everything from the royal treasury was distributed for free among the subjects, barring the exception of the ingredients of war? Perhaps no one could satisfy my query. Even there is no proper history of the Kumbh-mela, though lakhs of men and women undertake this crazy journey to the Sangam in search of the divine nectar. Some people say that Sankaracharya was the founder of this mela. As far as I know, Sankaracharya established his *maths* at four places—Shringeri, Dwarka, Puri and Joshimath. There is no mention of Prayag in this canon.

Speaking of history, let us examine Sankaracharya's position a little more closely. The saga is slightly political. More than eleven hundred years ago, the preachers of Islam were riding on the waves of the Arabian Sea and landing in India in frequent batches. In the guise of preaching the religion, it was designed to occupy the kingdoms. And the low-caste Hindus started converting to Islam in great numbers, just to be freed of the terrible oppression of the higher caste Hindus. They did not even have the right to pray, or to enter the temples. Islam showed them a liberal face. Here God was not displeased if the kings and the subjects prayed together in the mosque. It is then that Sankaracharya undertook to reform Hinduism. Islam believed in oneness of God. Sankaracharya also formulated his *kebaladvaitabad* where the Hindu God is also one. He introduced the worship of the Nirguna. Of course, this religious movement was progressive by nature. It served a purpose at that juncture of India's religious history. But today, it has become irrelevant.

***

A news spread that the parade ground had caught fire. When the fire was people's lifeline to counter the cold wave, it suddenly appeared in a devastating form. I got scared. Balaram lived in the parade ground. I had not visited him since that night. I rushed to the place and found to my relief that the tent of Balaram was standing intact. On seeing me, Balaram smiled and said, 'I knew my Thakur will come. He can't remain indifferent after getting the news. Your friend from the other side visits me every day and asks why your Thakur has not come. I reply that he will come when the time is ripe.'

It was easy to guess that he was talking of Shyama. She desired to strike a chord of friendship or companionship with me. But my middle class sense of values stood on the way. I could not properly respond to her feelings.

Balaram said, 'Yesterday we all went to your ashram. We were told that you leave for the city every day.'

I was surprised. They visited me in the ashram, but no one told me anything. The cold had got the better of Prahlad. He had fallen sick. Hence, Brajabala was pre-occupied, otherwise she would have given me the news.

I asked, 'Who else were there with you?

'All the four of them. Shyamadasi, her co-wife, co-wife's sister and her daughter. She said, 'If my co-wife does not accompany us, he won't see us. Ha ha ha.'

Balaram's laughter was pure and innocent. But I could not join in it.

He asked, 'Would you like to visit her, Thakur?'

'No, Balaram, it won't be proper.'

***

There was a resurgence in the fair. In between, it had temporarily broken up. Many people returned home. But now double the number had started pouring in. The cold wave had subsided. The sunny weather had started rejuvenating everyone. Everyday, new batches of sadhus were entering the fair from far-off lands on elephants and horses. For the first time, I saw naked Naga sanyasis galloping on horses with unsheathed swords. Their fearsome appearance commanded frightened respect. It was difficult to say when this custom originated. I heard that nudity was age-old. But the origin of the sword belonged to the fourteenth century when Balanandaji created an armed battalion of sadhus to protect other sadhus. It is rumoured that sometime they had even taken part in royal battles.

The crowd and the new batches of sadhus gave the mela a new lease of life. The new moon day was approaching. This was the day of *purna-kumbha* (full kumbh). Hence the rush of people would now keep building up.

One night Panchugopal asked me, 'You are a writer. Will you write everything that you saw here?'

'I might.'

'About me too?'

'Why not?'

There was no one around. Still Panchugopal lowered his voice and whispered, 'Then please write that if she comes back and tells me "Babamoni, forgive me", I will surely—'

His voice became choked with emotion. He left me with heavy footsteps. I did not know where his estranged daughter was. But if my appeal could move her, then I would surely write, 'Shiuli, where have you blossomed? Where are you spreading colour? Your father is roaming the earth for you like a mad wanderer. Please come and call him "Babamoni" once. That will soothe him.'

***

The Kumbh-mela suddenly turned crazy. The flood of people surpassed all that we had seen so far. It seemed as if the fair was bursting in its seams. I was concerned, for more people might spell disaster.

The new moon was approaching. In the morning, Balaram visited our tent and said, 'Come, Thakur.'

'Where, my dear?'

'The only destination that beckons you.'

The inmates of my ashram were scandalized to see the lame and unkempt Balaram. Such words were also circulating that I was in search of some secret charms and talisman, otherwise why should I rub shoulders with such lowly persons? Even Brajabala started distancing herself from me.

We started to walk. From the direction Balaram took, it was not difficult for me to guess where he was leading me to. From some distance, I could see Shyama standing in an isolated spot on the bank of the Yamuna. At her feet, there was a pitcher full of water. She had just taken a bath and was wearing a bright red sari. She must have seen me, yet she was standing with her face turned on the other side.

I slowed down and asked Balaram, 'You always sing of joy. Then why are you catalyzing this sorrowful relationship.'

Pat came Balaram's reply, 'Is not sorrow the other side of joy, Thakur? Otherwise, why do we cry in extreme pleasure?'

His logic was unbeatable. I walked towards Shyama. I was taken aback by seeing an agonized expression on her face, which was usually full of playfulness and banter. Instead of lightning, there was rain in her eyes. She gave me a sidelong glance and said, 'Liar!'

I had to accept the accusation since I had failed her. I did not keep my promise of meeting her again. I just smiled and said lamely, 'I heard you all came to my ashram the other day.'

Shyama's lips curled into a sarcastic smile, 'But you fled. Coward!'

I tried to reassure her saying, 'No, I had not fled. How would I know that you would visit our ashram?'

'You knew. But you escaped out of fear.'

'Fear of whom?'

'Fear of me. Who else?'

'Why should I be afraid of you?'

Shyama turned her face away and said in a pathetic tone, 'For I am a spoilt woman. I might trouble you. That's why you had not come even after promising. The mela being over, you will leave. I will also leave. But can't there be friendship between a man and a woman?'

Again, she turned to face me. Now the trademark flash of laughter was back in her face and eyes. She continued, 'If you had come, I would not have given you trouble. I am not as bad as you think.'

I knew that I was defeated. Shyama only desired my friendship. My heart wanted to reciprocate, but my social self stood in the way. Today, that curtain was also torn away. I felt as if Shyama's blood-red sari had turned blue. Must be the trick of the Yamuna. When did the sound of flute from the bank of the Yamuna care for people's approbation or public disgrace?

I said, 'Shyama, I am not a coward. I just did not want to hurt you further.'

Shyama laughed, '*Meri taklif* (my trouble)? You are a fool. Now listen, I will come here to bathe every day. Please come and meet me every day till we leave. Will you?'

Before I could reply, Balaram came to my rescue, though unwittingly. He said, 'I have learnt a Hindi song here. Would you like to listen, Thakur?'

Listen, O Radhe, don't go to the bank of Yamuna
At the bower of Vrindavan...

There was no difficulty for Shyama to understand the meaning of this song. She bent her head and looked at Balaram first and then at me. Then she smiled her mysterious smile and invited me, 'Come. Let's go.'

'Where?'

'At our place.'

I tagged along. Reaching there, I was amazed to see that Shyama took recourse to a blatant lie without batting an eyelid. She had met me on the way and brought me with her. The middle-aged Premavati smiled at me and said, 'We went to your ashram the other day. How long will you stay here?'

I replied politely, 'Thinking of staying till the new moon is over.'

Then my eyes met with the burning tiger eyes of the old man. He was staring at me. I started averting my eyes, but to my surprise, he suddenly flashed a toothless smile and asked, 'All well?'

I replied, 'Yes'.

The old man said, 'My youngest wife often talks of you. God bless you!'

With these words, he turned grave and heaved a deep sigh with his eyes fixed at the horizon.

After that, Shyama and I met almost every day. Not just on the bank of the river, but at the temple of Nag-Basuki, at the place of Benimadhav at Darganj, at the chickpea field on the other side of the Yamuna. Balaram was always with us. Even Premavati was also there once or twice.

On the day preceding the new moon, I declared on the bank of the Yamuna, 'I will leave day after tomorrow'.

Shyama quickly replied, 'We too.'

Looking at the river for a few moments, she asked, 'Will you remember?'

'What?'

'All this.'

'Yes, I will.'

She fixed me with a stinging sidelong glance and uttered her favorite epithet, 'Liar!'

Balaram butted in, 'Where is my gift, Thakur?'

I asked, 'What gift?'

He said, 'Well, one has to reward the go-between for arranging these meetings.'

Shyama laughed and said, 'I will give you a farewell gift. Tomorrow early morning. In front of Babuji.'

I could not go in the early morning. I got delayed for something or other. Suddenly, everyone in the ashram rushed out in the open. I found there was a huge crowd running helter and skelter. A big hue and cry could be heard from some distance. People were running like mad, some beating their chests and crying, some pulling at their hair and crying. It was learnt that there was a bloody incident. Thousands of people had been killed, some murdered, some succumbed to stampede. I also pushed forward to find out what exactly happened. Someone said that the intoxicated Naga sadhus had created a ruckus, which resulted in a stampede. Dead bodies were piled up in front of the temple of Hanuman-ji at the parade ground.

I could not cross the bridge immediately; the police had cordoned it off. It took me three hours of patient effort to reach the parade ground. But everything there was devastated. There was no trace of Balaram's tent, nor the cottage of Shyama. All around were corpses of men, women and children trampled, smashed and distorted. Colourful dupattas and silk saris, *nagra* chappals and embroidered kurtas, the necklaces hanging from necks and tiaras decorating the forehead, along with the torn clothes of the vagabonds—all were mingled together. But there was not a single body of a sadhu in that heap. People were trying to rush in, breaking the police cordon. They were searching for their mothers, wives, sons, daughters and other near and dear ones.

Somebody shouted, 'This is sheer murder. All by the drunk sadhus.' People's anger against the sadhus and the government officials had reached the boiling point.

I returned to the ashram. Many of our inmates had also got injured. A broken leg here, a disjointed hand there. But even in this condition, everyone had started packing. One day, all these people had madly rushed to the Kumbh-mela in search of the divine ambrosia. Today, another mad rush was there to leave the mela at the first opportunity.

Dusk fell. The sky of Prayag turned crimson by the fire rising from hundreds of pyres. One wondered why did the Kumbh turn so dreadful? Was it not supposed to be the source of piety? Or is it trying to expiate for the sin of humanity?

Panchugopal's entire entourage was leaving. No one called me or tried to find out what I wanted to do. Only Brajabala came at the last moment and asked, 'Aren't you coming?'

I picked up my shoulder bag and said, 'Yes. Let's go.'

However, I could not accompany them beyond the parade ground. It drew me like a magnet. But I could see only strangers and unknown faces. When I was about to give up, I suddenly saw Lakshmidasi sitting under a tree. She was accompanied by a few badly ruffled Vaishnavas from her camp.

Seeing me, Lakshmidasi said in a calm and composed voice, 'How many times have I warned him, Thakur? But how can I take back someone who came here to leave for the other world?'

'What happened?'

One of her companions pointed towards a pyre and said, 'He is there.'

I was dumbstruck. Balaram came here with his garden of flowers. His gardener was now left behind alone. I managed to control myself with supreme effort.

After some time, I asked, 'Shouldn't we make a move?'

She replied, 'Let the fire of the pyre extinguish, Thakur.'

I did not object. After a long time, I asked hesitantly, 'Do you know anything about the others?'

She replied, 'I have not seen your friend. But I have seen her co-wife beating her chest and crying inconsolably. I dared not ask anything.'

This could mean only one thing. But I was so stunned by Balaram's death that I did not feel any additional grief.

We sat through the night looking at the embers of the pyre. At daybreak, we made a move. We joined the great mass of people running away from death and devastation.

At the station, we were looking for space in every compartment when someone called. It was the oldest wife of the deceased polygamist. I got up with Lakshmidasi. She was offered a seat near Premavati. Next to her was Shyama. She had covered her whole face with a white modesty scarf.

The oldest wife said, 'Our old man passed away, Babuji.'

All the women started sobbing. Only Shyama's reaction was not visible.

There was no room to sit. So, I sat down on our luggage. Suddenly, I noticed that Shyama's head cover had fallen off and she was staring at me. There was no vermillion on the parting of her hair, there was no dotted mark on her forehead. Perhaps that was the beginning of her widowhood. There was pain and fatigue on her face, maybe due to the bereavement, maybe due to the sleepless night, but did I spot a suppressed relief, even happiness, in her face? After looking straight at me for a long moment, she cast her eyes down.

After a long time, perhaps I also dozed off like the others. I woke up at a cold touch on my arm. It was Shyama. Her lips quivered as she whispered, 'We will get down at Patna soon to board another train.'

Without thinking I asked, 'Why?'

She smiled sorrowfully and said, 'That's the way to reach home.'

Without any hesitation, I turned around to face her and said, 'Balaram—'

She said, 'I know. You did not come to the riverbank in the morning. I gave him something on your behalf.'

'What?'

'One of my rings.'

I kept looking at her, dumbfounded.

She again flashed a sad smile and said, 'Tell me something. What do you think of me?'

'Couldn't form any opinion yet.'

'But I've formed my opinion about you.'

'What's that?'

'You are heartless.'

How would I react to this accusation? Balaram was no longer with me. Otherwise, he would have given a befitting reply through a song. Only he perhaps knew that I was not a liar, nor was I heartless.

The train reached Patna station. The old woman said, 'We are leaving, Babuji.' Premavati also said, 'Bye.' Shyama's lips quivered a little. Did she say anything? At least I did not hear. All of them got down at the platform in a huddle. I could not utter a single word of leave-taking. I just kept looking at Shyama like a dumb person.

My passenger train halted at every station and reached Burdwan the next morning. It was a journey of almost forty hours. I had to catch a connecting train from here. Lakshmidasi also got down. Before leaving, she touched my feet and said, 'Thakur!'

'Yes?'

I was surprised that she started humming a song. She had such a sweet voice. But it had to be. After all, she was Balaram's guru. She sang:

No one saw the fire burning in my mind
There is fire in the wind set by the tune of your flute

It invokes Falgun at any time
You roamed by playing on your flute
But my mind missed it

As she sang with her eyes shut, tears streamed down her cheeks. Today, the chief of the *akhra* was crying at the loss of her lead singer and soulmate.

My train arrived. I had to leave. I had taken the voyage in search of the nectar. Today, I did not know what I had brought back. I had only memories of a host of people, the variety of Nature's creation. I was remembering all the faces, as I started walking through the village after alighting from the train.

It was noontime. I had to cross Bagdipara, the area of low-caste people, to reach my home. Suddenly someone called, 'Are you back, son? Please wait for a moment.'

It was the old Abala Bagdini. Why did she ask me to wait? I was already very tired. She returned with a pitcher full of water on her hip and said, 'Take off your shoes.'

'Why?'

'Please do as I tell you.'

I did as told. She poured all the water from the pitcher on my feet and washed it saying, 'You have returned from the pilgrimage. It is our custom to wash the feet of such a person.'

The touch of the cold water soothed my entire body. My eyes became misty in rapture.

Where does one's journey end? Back home, Abala Bagdini gave me an intimation of a new source of nectar. The search never ends.

GLOSSARY

avadhut – one of a class of anchorites who worship Shiva

akhra – a place where Vaishnavas assemble for religious worship and singing kirtan

amrut – guava

anchal/pallu – the loose end of a draped sari the loose end of a draped sari, sometimes used to veil one's face and head

awara – vagabond

bakshish – tip / a sum of money given to someone as a reward for a service

bol – notation of music

baiji – professional dancing girl and songstress

bori – sun-dried lentil balls, often in the shape of dumplings

brahmacharii (man) / *brahmacharini* (woman) – one who has attained knowledge about gods, and practices sexual abstinence

byas – an expression of exasperation usually, equivalent to 'Enough!' or 'Is that all?' or 'That's all!'

chakra – the circle in which sanyasis sit to perform a secret esoteric ritual

chandal – someone who deals with disposal of corpses, traditionally considered to be untouchable

charanamrita – the water with which the feet of a deity or a revered person has been washed

dom – a lower-caste Bengali Hindu, who are known to be associated with the cremation of the dead and looking after the crematorium; the *dom* women used to serve as village midwives

daktar-babu – 'daktar' is for 'doctor'; 'babu' is a respectful title or form of address for a man, especially an educated one

dokta – tobacco leaf for chewing

hathyogi – a sect of yogis who specialize in yogic acrobatics

Hindiwala – a term for the North Indians, who speak Hindi; slightly derogatory in tone

jhola – a cloth bag

kapali – a low-born Hindu woman

kapalik – an ascetic worshipping the cult of Godess Kali in an awful manner

Kapalkundala and Nabakumar – Heroine and hero of Bankimchandra's iconic novel, *Kapalkundala*; she guides Nabakumar, a young city-bred man who lost his way in the jungle. Foster-daughter of a tantrik kapalik, she later saves him from the clutches of the kapalik and elopes with Nabakumar to the city.

Krishna-*leela* – 'leela' means dalliance/activities; the anecdotes and narratives of Krishna's life are generally titled as Krishna-*leela*

kuleen – an upper-caste Hindu belonging to any of the families on whom an order of honour was conferred by King Ballal Sen of ancient Bengal; often members of such families practised polygamy, and here, that is what has been referred to in the context of Bhuihars

maharaj – literally means king; but also used to address superior person, specially in the religious parlance

maund – a measure of weight, prevalent in India, before the introduction of the metric system; sightly less in weight them 40 kilograms

meherbaan – kind, generous

moomphali – peanuts with shell

nagra chappals – footwear, with its head resembling the hood of a *naag* or snake

namavali – piece of cloth printed with names of gods, usually Lord Krishna or Lord Rama

odhni – dupatta / a length of cloth worn over the chest and thrown back around the shoulders, typically with a salwar kameez, by women from South Asia

peda – a kind of sweetmeat prepared by solidifying cow-milk

rickshawala – rickshaw-puller / the driver of a cycle rickshaw

sadhak/sadhika – a worshipper, a devotee

stotra – in Sanskrit, an ode, eulogy or a hymn of praise

thakur – a reverential address to a superior person or a male god

KINSHIP TERMS

bhaiya – big brother

bouthan – elder brother's wife

dada – elder brother

dadababu/dadabhai – an address to someone as respectable as one's elder brother; also used to address one's employer or master

didima – generally, maternal grandmother; also a term for addressing an old woman who might be of one's grandmother's age

di'ma – a corrupt and affectionate form of the above

khurhi – aunt; father's younger brother's wife

pishi – aunt; father's sister